AN *unforgettable* JOURNEY

*From the Doors of a Church
to the Security Gates of a Prison*

JANENE PRUDLER

Recharge Ministries Publishing Company
New Mexico

An Unforgettable Journey
From the Doors of a Church
to the Security Gates of a Prison

Janene Prudler

ISBN: 978-0-578-73083-7
Recharge Ministries Publishing Company
New Mexico

Cover design: Amy Grigoriou
Page layout & pre-press: Lighthouse24

Contents

Foreword

WHEN MY SISTER asked me to write her foreword for this book, I felt both honored and privileged to share my thoughts with you, about my sister, my hero. Janene's unforgettable journey, for me, started when she was sixteen years old as I watched her fight to survive a devastating illness that nearly took her life. She never gave up the fight to survive, and I see that same determination in everything she does. Her love for the Lord refuses to leave anyone behind if given an opportunity to touch someone's life for Christ. The unforgettable journey she is on today has taken her from co-pastoring a church to the security gates of a prison.

You may ask, "Why prison ministry?" Bob and Janene both lived a past that allows them to identify with those who are incarcerated. Her published biography called "Good Girl Bad Girl, My Father's

Daughter" tells the story of her life and the God who chose to forgive her. When they stand before the prisoners to minister, those who have read her book are encouraged and given hope knowing if God can transform her and Bob's life, he can also do it for them.

They continue to demonstrate a love for the prisoners and will walk into any prison that the Lord opens for them. In the forty-five years of their ministry they have ministered from the East Coast to the West Coast. Bob has traveled and ministered in the countries of El Salvador, Brazil, and Mexico as well as helping to establish two churches while in India. Though they spent thirty-eight years as pastors both Bob and Janene know that God, in these last days of their lives, have called them to minister to prisoners. They walk into prison knowing that they are seeing every prisoner with the same eyes as Jesus sees them. If you knew my sister you would hear her say many times, "We love our guys in orange."

Our family is a witness to the hundreds of lives that have been changed through their ministry. You will not be disappointed when you open the pages of this book and experience Janene's "Unforgettable Journey."

Acknowledgements

I HAVE BEEN ASKED many times how long it takes to write a book. My first reaction to that question is, if you knew what is involved and the commitment it takes, you may want to reconsider. My last two books took two years each to finish. I have read many Christian novels by authors who have written multiple books and thought to myself, how is that even possible.

When it comes to writing an inspirational Christian book, I invite the Holy Spirit into every page. My words alone cannot change hearts and accomplish the purpose for which they were written. Knowing how every word has the ability to speak into someone's life, puts a tremendous responsibility on me as a Christian author. When each manuscript is finished and ready for print, I have a hard time writing my name as the author when the title really belongs to the Holy Spirit.

I would be remiss not to recognize those who have helped make this book ready for publication. One of the most important aspects of writing a book is to have the encouragement of those around you. I have been blessed to have those in my family help me through the reading and rereading of the manuscript, checking for any errors or suggestions. My daughter Leah Ashurst always stopped what she was doing to read every chapter I would drop off to her. My husband Bob, who would finish his video ministry long enough to read through the manuscript and offer his advice. My son Aaron Prudler, who agreed to do the final reading and corrections before sending my work to Lighthouse24 to be formatted for publication.

A special thanks to my granddaughter Cristee Ashurst, who drew several illustrations to highlight some of the chapter titles in this book. We could not have touched as many prisoners without Stephnie and Chris Geiman who were on our team. Never have we worked with two such amazing people who loved the prisoners as much as we did.

Introduction

"When God Closes One Door,
He Open's Another"

TWO YEARS AGO, I walked into my office and laid a paper on my computer with the words, An Unforgettable Journey. I was certain at the time that I knew why the Lord had dropped those three words into my heart. My mornings belonged to the Lord and during our time together I would visualize this amazing spiritual journey I longed to experience with Him. There were days I understood what it meant to dwell in His courts not wanting to leave His presence. I knew there was more, and I wanted all of it. I longed for a deeper understanding of what it truly meant to love the Lord with all my heart, soul, and mind.

My passion for more was inspired by my first book written and published in 2013 called, "God's Path to Intimacy." From the moment I held that book in my hands, I chose to live out the truths found within it, which were inspired by the Holy Spirit. I was not only ready to experience this journey with the Father, but to write about our time together. I walked back to my office later that day ready to put pen to paper, confident that I now had the title to this book. I started to write the introduction page and pulled out a few scriptures I wanted to lead with. I found myself staring at the paper in front of me throughout most of the day until I realized this was not the journey God intended for my life. I struggled with how to interpret this change in what I was feeling. Was it possible that everything I had anticipated and envisioned over the last few months would become an unfulfilled desire? If not on a spiritual journey, where was He taking me?

There were many mornings I spoke these words

to the Lord found in Proverbs 16:9 "A man's heart plans his way, but the Lord directs his steps." Perhaps in this situation I found myself in, it could read, He interrupts our plans in order to set His plans into motion. That is exactly what He chose to do, and I was not invited to be a part of the planning session. In fact, this journey He was about to take me on was nothing I could have anticipated. I was unable to see the complete picture until I arrived at His final destination for my life. The road felt rocky many times as I was only allowed to see one day at a time.

It would prove to be an unforgettable journey and it started ten-years ago when God chose to close a door for me that would alter my life forever. I was not ready or prepared for what I had no voice in. During the next eight years I would experience what I thought was one disappointment after another as I watched doors continually close for me. My life was ministry and every attempt I made to minister seemed to be a picture of failure.

Until one day, when I understood that He had directed my steps and controlled the circumstances of my life for the last eight years to bring me to His final destination for my life before calling me home. Looking back, I realize that every disappointment I experienced was a part of His greater plan to bring me to a place I would perfectly fit in.

I hope this book will encourage you to step out and believe for God's greater plan for your life.

-1-

My Unforgettable Journey
Its Beginning

WHILE SITTING AT MY DESK reading my Bible one morning enjoying the warmth of the sunshine coming through my office window, I happened to pause to reflect on what had been on my heart for months. I was longing for a depth of communion with the Lord that I had not yet experienced. I would envision this image of a passport stamped inside with amazing spiritual places I traveled during my devotional times with the Lord. While directing those thoughts to Heaven, I happened to look up and notice two plaques that had been hanging on my wall above me. They were plaques that represented my twenty-five years of ministry within the denomination I served under that were given to honor those years. Since the day I hung them up, I never felt the need to look at them again. I serve an All-Knowing God and I knew the pages of His book told the story of my life.

Before leaving my office that morning I felt a tugging on my heart that I was being called to start writing a book titled, "An Unforgettable Journey." I was certain the Lord had dropped the title of this book into my heart one morning during my devotional time with Him. Knowing myself well, I stopped and walked to my office that day and wrote the title down and placed it on my computer so as not to forget it. I went back to finish my time with the Lord but found it hard to focus. I later walked back to my office anxious to put pen to paper. I had the title of the book and the vision of what the finished cover would look like. Or so I thought!

Man makes plans but God orders our steps, or should I say, He interrupts our plans in order to set His plans into motion. I went on believing I had the complete picture that God was painting for me. I spent months googling images searching for the perfect passport I felt would fit the cover of what I believed this book was supposed to be. It was a vision that I saw for months but suddenly the vision was gone, and another took its place. Where was God taking me, and what would it take for me to arrive at His appointed destination for my life?

I knew where I needed to start, and where this journey first began for me. I thought I was preparing myself for this amazing spiritual adventure only to realize a few paragraphs into my writing that God had other plans for my life and for this book. Would my passport no longer look like what I had envisioned for months and longed to experience?

The year was 2010 and circumstances not in my control brought my husband and I to the end of being Senior Pastors after thirty-eight years. Fulltime ministry was no longer an option as Bob was facing several surgeries and felt he was unable to give the time it took to oversee a church. Though I certainly understood his decision, it left me with one question I would continue to ask myself. What about me and where do I fit into this picture? It left me with an empty feeling that I no longer had a place to belong. I would continue to struggle for months believing there was nothing left for me. Ministry was all I had known and what I felt defined my life.

Bob and I had established churches from the West Coast to the East Coast. We were ministry partners working together before the ink even dried on our marriage license. My gift was administration and from the start of our ministry I was driven to make sure all aspects of church life ran as I thought they should. I was numbered among many Christians who continue for years believing that what we were doing was pleasing to the Lord. My way of thinking at the time was, why wouldn't the Lord be pleased with the years that I made certain we had the best programs and met all the needs of the church?

I continued this work-oriented pace for the years we were pastors until the day the Lord stepped in, and I was no longer in control of the circumstances that were about to affect my life. It felt like a death to everything I lived for and was not ready to give up. I never stopped long enough to question God as to what His plan for my life was now that church ministry was no longer an option for me. For the first time Bob and I were no longer a team. I found myself with no voice in any of the decisions that were being made.

While I was grieving my lost opportunity to be involved in ministry, God was working behind the scenes and the curtain was soon to be lifted. There would be many scenes behind that very curtain before I would see the complete picture God was painting for me at that time in my life. We have often heard the comment that others often see in us what we cannot see for ourselves. In my situation, I was unable to see what only the eyes and heart of God could see in me.

What happens when all is stripped away? Where do we turn and to whom should we turn to? I was going to learn something about myself that I never stopped long enough to see. It would not be an overnight revelation, but it would be a revelation straight from the heart of God. While I laid out before Him all that I had done over the years, His response to me was, "I never asked you to do any of that." *Galatians 3:3 "Are you so foolish? Having begun in the Spirit, are now made perfect by the flesh?"* My service lay in fleshly outward performances. Where the flesh is permitted to influence our service for God, it soon results in open sin.

If I recall my reaction to those words, it would be more of an instant eye opener into the depth of my personality. Though it was hard to hear, I knew it to be the truth. My personality has always been the drive behind most everything I do in life. I thrive on productivity and never need to look far at what needs to be done.

There are circumstances that seem to unfold in our lives that we are often unable to recognize until those defining moments where clarity is finally revealed and we say, "I get it!" We were soon to see a bigger picture of what the Lord had planned for our lives. Though full-time ministry was not an option, Bob felt a stirring in his heart to make himself available to churches for meetings. For us to launch out into uncharted territory we would have to establish our own 501c3 ministry with the IRS. In 2010 Recharge Ministries was established and has been active ever since.

It was not long before my gift of administration found a purpose in this new call on our lives. I was soon needed to design and prepare packets to distribute to the different churches. Was this going to be enough to fill the void I still felt after leaving church ministry behind? No! Looking back, I began to envision some type of ministry that would bring the fulfillment I was looking for. I soon felt a stirring in my heart to start a woman's seminar on "The Father Heart of God." Little did I know at the time that the Father was very much involved in what I thought was my choice of topics. I could not possibly have seen His hand in all of this for many months.

I was anxious to start working on what I felt the Lord was directing me to teach on. I knew the most important material I would need was right in my own office. I found myself pulling out all my own personal resources. I continued to search the web on any books that spoke about the Heavenly Father and ordered them. I had finished designing the brochure and had chosen several session topics and was eager to start my research. I remember setting up a separate table that allowed me to lay out my books and computer.

It was not difficult for me to prepare each night, and I was excited about the material that was developing. Since my office was also in my bedroom it was more convenient for me to do my studying in a corner of the living room away from everyone. I have never been good at focusing on what I am doing if there is even the least bit of noise. There was only one problem that presented itself night after night, and it was critical to what I was about to teach in the coming months.

Most of my studying was done in the evenings and those were the times I would start to question what I was thinking when choosing this subject. Did I really believe this seminar was inspired by the Lord? Every night I found myself stopping long enough to look up as though the Father was just a few feet away and I would say to Him, "How can I possibly teach on the "Father Heart of God." Night after night I would point to my head and say to Him, "Why can't I get it from my head to my heart that You love me?" Never did I get an answer, and I understand now that I had too many scars holding me back from hearing what I needed to hear. Though I never once questioned the Saviors love, I would continue to struggle with identifying with the Father part of the Triune God.

Nevertheless, I continued to prepare for this seminar, knowing the date I set was drawing near. With that knowledge came a sudden feeling of fear and confusion. The words that daily occupied my brain were, "How am I to speak about a Father who doesn't love me?" How could He? I was ashamed of my past. I continued to struggle with the love I wanted so desperately from Him. Was the Father about to prove His love for me through circumstances that went way beyond anything I could have imagined?

Some of you will have already read portions of the next few paragraphs in my second book, "Good Girl Bad Girl, My Father's Daughter." Those that have can understand my struggles in identifying with the Father. The effects of a fatherless life and home were scars I carried for years. I felt it was necessary to add a few of those paragraphs in this book for those who may not have read my story. Little did I realize at the time that God was at work destroying any doubts I previously had about His love. The Father was going to make certain I received my answer in ways that no one else could get the glory for, and that I would never question His love again.

-2-

The Father's Love

Short Inserted From
"Good Girl Bad Girl My Father's Daughter"

While in Michigan to say goodbye to my natural father for the last time I decided to do some shopping with my sister-in-law. It was not that we were necessarily poor, but we both loved to shop at any thrift store we could find open. On this particular day, I walked in the store and headed straight for the used book section. Flying on trips did not leave much room in my suitcase for big items, but I always had room for a book or two. I reached for a book called; "Created to be God's Friend" by Henry Blackaby. It was written about the life of the Patriarch Abraham and how he became God's friend.

I flew home and started to read the book, and by the time I finished, my struggle to see myself as someone the Heavenly Father could love was over. I had flown two thousand miles to say goodbye to my birth father and instead, the Holy Spirit lead me to a book that opened my heart and eyes to the Heavenly Father's love.

I was content and at peace knowing that I was assured of the Father's, love and could lead the women's seminar with confidence. I had everything I needed to fill the void I once felt. I had the Father's love and a ministry that would make me feel complete. Little did I know that this was only the beginning of what the Father had planned for my life. Looking back, I realize I could not possibly fulfill what He would continually ask of me if I did not trust in His love.

I thought I was going right back home to make the seminars available to other churches and felt certain that doors would soon be opened to me. My brochures were quality and I included them in my husband's packets to the different churches. Yet, no future doors were opened to me, and I struggled once again to understand why. Looking back, I sincerely believe if doors had been open at that time, it would have silenced the voice of God and stopped any plans He had for my life. A plan I would not comprehend, for several years.

It was clear that doors were not flying open requesting my ministry gift when I returned home. It was easier to convince myself that when God closes one door, He opens another. David Kykes says, "Sometimes our disappointments in life can become God's appointments, so don't let closed doors bother you." I was looking at my closed door as another failure on my part. You start to question yourself and say, "Was that really You God?" This is not the outcome I imagined when I started this assignment. It felt like everything I set my heart to do, eventually ended in disappointment.

Looking back, I can see how I was feeding this constant void in my life with any form of spiritual activity. I never once acknowledged or understood at the time that God was responsible for closing the door. Instead, I accepted it as a picture of my past failures. I realize now that much of my past contributed to how I continued to interpret life at that time.

I was unable to let go of wanting to somehow feel used of God. I knew that the Father understood my every thought before it was ever voiced. I wondered if there was something more for me to do. It did not take long for Him to answer. While sitting at my computer allowing my imagination to envision once again what I might do to fill my time I heard this, "I want you to write a book on the

Tabernacle of Moses." None of this made sense to me at the time. My response to Him was, I am not sure I heard You right. You are asking me to write about something I know so little about. If He would have shown me at the time how this assignment was going to forever change my life, I would never have left my computer until the book was written and published.

Imagine one day your sitting in your office with no thought of becoming an author when you hear a voice say, "I want you to write a book." You have no concept of where to start other than picking up paper and pencil. You face the truth that you are not an educated person. Everything you know is what you have had to teach yourself. Spell check on your computer suddenly becomes your lifesaver and closest friend. You immediately realize you cannot do this without help. You spend moments where you want to silently argue with God while trying to convince Him He has made a huge mistake.

I came to realize with this assignment that God would never ask me to do something I was able to accomplish without Him. My knowledge of the Tabernacle of Moses was so limited. Though I had read the Bible through several times, I had never spent any time studying that portion of scripture. If I were going to write a book on the Tabernacle, I would certainly need to spend hours researching while trusting that the Holy Spirit would teach me what I needed to know. If the Bible were written by men inspired by the Holy Spirit, I could confidently move forward knowing that He would impart His wisdom into my life in this book.

For the next two years I would sit at my desk writing and rewriting portions of my notes. It became difficult at times when I felt like day after day, I was merely getting small pieces of what this book was to look like. Was I mistaken in what I thought God had said? I knew I was looking for a way out of what seemed to consume so much of my life every day. Each time those thoughts entered my mind, I knew I was again questioning the voice of the Lord. What if He did tell me to write this book and I chose not to? I have always had this respectful fear of the Lord that held me back from making mistakes when it came to His voice speaking into my life. Those were the moments that I knew I had no choice but to continue to write.

What developed out of this assignment after nearly two years was my first published book called, "God's Path to Intimacy." When it came time to publish it, I struggled putting my own name as the author. How foolish of us to think that we can change any life apart from the Holy Spirit. He was the true author and deserved to be acknowldeged.

Was publishing God's Path to Intimacy what changed my life? No! Like so many other written books, they are of no value unless one chooses to pick them up and read them. Many books are written by anointed men and women that will simply remain on bookshelves, set aside for perhaps another time. Upon receiving my first copy of "God's Path to Intimacy" it became my choice as to what I would do with the book I now held in my hands. Would it be enough that I was now considered a published author? Perhaps I opened the book impressed with what I had accomplished with the help of the Holy Spirit. I spent most of my life looking for recognition, and never dreamed it would come as a result of "God's Path to Intimacy."

My dream of self-accomplishment was not what God had in mind. Recognition would not come from publishing "God's Path to Intimacy." The Father's plan for my life had nothing to do with self, and instead it became a very humbling experience that I would be asked to write such a powerful life changing book. Was this writing assignment the fulfillment of God's intended purpose for my life, or was it the catalyst for yet another piece of the puzzle in this journey He has me on?

-3-

The Path of Life

Seek God's will in All you Do and
He will show you the path to take.

MANY MORNINGS, I would remind myself of these words from **Proverbs 16:9** that says, **"A man's heart makes plans, but it's God who directs his steps."** My unforgettable journey did not come to an end after having published "God's Path to

Intimacy." In fact, the path God had designed for my life was nothing I could foresee at the time. My mornings were set aside for Him alone, and if there was to be more that He wanted for my life, He would reveal it in His time through the Holy Spirit.

It was during one of those prayerful moments with the Lord that I felt I needed to set aside a time to fast. I considered the Holy Spirit my best friend and knew fasting would cause me to be more sensitive to hearing His voice. I arranged to go to a cabin in the mountains where I knew I would not be disturbed. I spent three days praying while fasting all food.

By day three I was weak and ready to return home. I woke up the following morning with no preconceived thoughts as to what might have been the result of my fast. I do remember sitting on the floor attempting to offer acceptable worship to the Lord with my guitar, happy that He was not looking for perfection. It was during those attempts that I heard the Holy Spirit say, "I want you to write your biography." I found myself unable to understand why He would ask me to write a book about my life.

I had always thought if I were to write another book, it would be called "I'm the Kings Cupbearer." Never could I imagine that instead, I would be asked to write my biography. I remained on the floor that morning for what seemed like hours trying to comprehend the reason behind His request. He was not obligated to lay out His whole plan just so I could agree to it. He was challenging me to step out in faith regardless of my inability to understand what He was asking of me at the time. **Proverbs 3:5 "Trust in the Lord with all your heart and lean not unto your own understanding."** No problem, I had no understanding to lean on at the time.

It was not until I finally received a clear vision of why I was being asked to write my story that I was able to move forward with this assignment. My biography would explain why I struggled as a Christian, believing that I could be loved by the

Heavenly Father. I would spend months going back into my childhood and remembering things I had long put to rest. I never once imagined that there was a higher purpose in publishing my story, but there was. I just did not know at the time what that was. **Ephesians 3:20 "Now to Him who is able to do exceedingly abundantly above all we ask or imagine."**

It would take me two years to complete the writing of my second book called "Good Girl, Bad Girl, My Father's Daughter." When I opened myself up to fasting in order to hear from the Holy Spirit, I could never have imagined what the outcome of that fast would mean. A few days after I received my first copy of "Good Girl Bad Girl my Father's Daughter," I sat down to search through my address book for the names of those who had ordered my book. When I opened the first page, I found myself looking at the name of a girl I knew, who was incarcerated in a Texas prison. Before I could take my eyes off the page, it was as though I heard the voice of the Lord say, "Who do you think needs this book?" I immediately knew what the answer was. I went to the computer that afternoon and filled out an application to become a volunteer with Prison Fellowship.

I was given thirty days in which to complete the application process. Having finished the requirements and testing, I received a call from Prison Fellowship's representative, who had oversight over New Mexico, Arizona, and Nevada at the time. We made plans to meet, and I felt a real draw and desire to help in any way I could. Shortly after our meeting, I was given an opportunity to be a part of a team going into the Douglas, Arizona Men's Prison to do quarterly weekend seminars.

I still remember the day our ministry team was scheduled to do a weekend seminar. It would be my first time as a volunteer and my first into a prison. We pulled up to the security yard gate, showed them our licenses, while assuring them that our phones were shut off. We were then directed to pull up to a designated area where we were each asked to step out of the car while the guard and his dog searched through our vehicle. Once we were cleared, we made our way to the prisons Mohave Unit. This unit is a high security prison for those convicted in the state of Arizona. I felt excited, yet I had a sense of apprehension about what to expect once we entered inside the prison walls. I followed the rest of our team through security and eventually we were able to set up for our seminar in the prison chapel.

Though this was my first time into a prison, I felt no fear. I was confident knowing that most of our team had been doing these seminars for years. The prisoners that signed up to attend chapel that day began to arrive and were given a name tag. Our sessions included worship, teaching, and an opportunity for the men to break off into small groups for discussions throughout the day. Smaller groups allowed the prisoners to share their thoughts about the different teachings being presented. This would be a two-day seminar which provided us with an opportunity to establish a more personal relationship with the prisoners when we returned the following day. When our two days were completed, we walked out of security knowing we would never forget the time we had with each of them. We would all look forward to returning for the next quarterly seminar.

During one of our team visits to the Douglas prison, I was given an opportunity to share my testimony and the reason I became a prison volunteer after writing "Good Girl Bad Girl, My Father's Daughter." As we were packing up our equipment, one of the prisoners handed me a sheet of paper containing the names of thirty-five prisoners requesting a copy of my book. With no time to think, I slipped that paper in my pocket as we continued to get ready to leave. I was later able to personally send thirty-five of both my first and second books to the names that were written on that piece of paper.

It was after a few visits going into the Douglas Prison that I was asked if I would be willing to lead the team. I had just become a volunteer and felt humbled and surprised to be considered so soon. I assume the decision was partly based on my thirty-eight years of pastoral ministry with my husband. Our team leader had been leading the team for twenty years and was wanting to work with Prison Fellowship's Angel Tree Ministry with his wife.

Plans were made to gather at a restaurant for our last planning session for the upcoming seminar. We all ordered our food and sat down to eat when the announcement was made that I would be their new team leader. Until that night none of our team were aware of the changes being made. Sitting beside me was a very capable woman who had been leading worship with the Douglas Team for years. When it was communicated that I would now be responsible to lead our team, it was as though I could sense her hurt without her saying a word. For several moments no one said anything. I am sure they could empathize with what she was feeling at that moment. I was the new kid on the block, and here I was being asked to lead this seasoned team. After the meeting I walked back to my car carrying the burden of what she must have felt when that announcement was made.

I realized after our next visit to the prison that this situation was not going to go away. There was a resistance that could be felt among our team and I did not help it any. I certainly understood the hurt she felt and found it best to step back from the ministry opportunity as a team leader. I wondered if it was possible to even feel comfortable going back to be a part of the team. It forced me to question whether I had heard the voice of the Lord concerning my continued involvement in prison ministry.

I knew I could expect a call over the situation from Nathan who is our Prison Fellowship's Leader. Nathan has a way of showing us how we might have handled things differently when it comes to ministry differences. I certainly felt I did not deal with the situation the way I should have. I continued to struggle with what I would say to Nathan when he called. My experience with the Douglas prisoners was beyond amazing, and my love for them made the thought of giving up being a part of the team more of a sacrifice then I felt I was willing to make.

I was hurt and angry with myself for the lost opportunity to be a part of prison ministry. I remember sitting on the floor in my office having coffee and reading my Bible the morning I knew I would be receiving the call from Nathan. I had set the phone next to me knowing he would be asking me what my plans for future prison minister were. He had set an approximate time to talk with me, and I was expecting his call at any moment. For two days I prayed and sought to understand if God's plan for my life included prison ministry. I knew I needed an answer that morning. I was not one to Bible search as I would follow chapter by chapter verse by verse in whichever book I happened to be in each day. I had finished the Old Testament that morning and had turned to Hebrews thirteen where I had left my Bible marker. When I read the words in verse three, **"Remember the prisoners as though you were chained to them,"** I knew I had heard the voice of the Lord through scripture. I received my answer the morning I needed to have it.

If you are ever tempted to doubt the Lord's ability to hear your heart in response to prayer, perhaps you might want to rethink that. Out of all the years reading my Bible, it was not a coincidence that I was in Hebrews thirteen that morning. The very day I needed to have an answer, God provided it. What a display of His personal love for me.

-4-

One Door Closes, Another Opens

GOD NEVER SHUTS
ONE DOOR
without
OPENING ANOTHER

I WAS NOW CERTAIN that prison ministry was a call God had placed on my life. Over the next few months, I would learn what it meant to wait on the Lord. I never went back to be a part of the Douglas team and would continue to struggle for months without having the opportunity to visit with the prisoners one more time. I wanted them to know the impact they made on my life for the short time I was there.

When God closes one door, He opens another. It was Several months later that I received a call from Nathan asking me to apply to take a team into one of the men's prisons in Safford, Arizona. It would only be a one-day seminar, but I was thrilled for the open door and opportunity to be back in prison ministry. Though the requirements for first time volunteers in Safford called for a few more details than ministering in the Douglas Prison, I was not going to turn down the opportunity. My first assignment was to gather a team and request the personal information that needed to be sent to the prison chaplain for security purposes. I made a call to Chris and Stephnie who were on the same team as I was in Douglas, and both had the heart for prison ministry. My son Aaron agreed to do the worship, and I felt confident that I now had a team I could count on.

Prison chaplains are there to help volunteers work through the requirements for each prison we volunteer in. I contacted Chaplain L. who I would be working through. It is my responsibility as team leader to gather and submit a detailed list of materials we would like to bring with us for ministry. It was not uncommon for one or more of the items listed to be disallowed such as an extra set of guitar strings, or unnecessary equipment cords. Our list would need to be approved through the prison captain.

Once we were given the clearance, a date was set for us to go into the Graham Complex in Safford. We arrived at the parking lot where we were met by Graham's Chaplain. We gathered our equipment while following him towards the security gate. He reassured us that there would be no problem with us getting through security. We all felt as if we had known this chaplain for years even though we had just met him that morning.

We continued to follow the chaplain through a few security gates before placing all our items on a table for inspection. Security is always going to be a priority when anyone enters a prison. Not only are we responsible to have prior clearance on the list of materials we plan on bringing in to minister, we can expect to be met by a guard who will search through our approved list while asking us mandatory security questions. Questions that we would hear repeatedly. We placed all our equipment on the table including any necessary items that needed to be removed from us personally before walking through the metal detector.

Detectors are there to make certain we are not carrying any contraband on us. We were each familiar with what to expect when it comes to prison security. What I have had to adapt to is the differences in sensitivities to the metals that each scanner is able to pick up at each prison. It is not always convenient and can be frustrating at times for me. I have had to learn by experience which prison scanners will detect my hair barrettes, and require me to remove them, and which ones will allow me to keep them on. The shoes and belt are usually always the first things that need to be removed. I should not complain, as I have watched guards required to comply with the same standards when entering any of the prisons.

Once our team was cleared, we were able to follow the chaplain through several more locked gates before entering the yard. Graham's Chaplain continued to communicate with us as we walked the distance to the chapel. It would be impossible to forget the rapport we felt with this chaplain. Those qualities set the stage for our team to minister with confidence that day. Throughout the day we saw such an amazing love this chaplain displayed for the prisoners he served.

Making a Difference

Whenever we have an open door into any prison for the first time, it is important to introduce our team members. We are there at the invitation of the chaplain and we humbly consider ourselves the invited guest of the prisoners. We are virtually walking into their space and they know nothing about us. This is their home and we can be certain that they will be making their own assumptions, about us.

Let me tell you a story.

I will always consider it a blessing to be gifted with a team that walks into any prison with a sense of humility. Let me explain. Each one of us has had an undesirable past that we have been redeemed from. The prisoners will learn through our testimonies that we are not there to judge them. We hope the changes brought about in our lives will encourage the prisoners that God has a plan for each of them regardless of their past.

My team members Chris and Stephnie were able to share a little of their background and what God had brought them through. I was able to share a portion of my testimony and how I became a prison volunteer through the book I wrote. This led one of the prisoners to ask me how he could order my book. Prisoners make so little money with the job they do in prison, and I did not want him to order it off Amazon. When all the prisoners had left the chapel that day, I turned to Graham's Chaplain and asked if I could send a few of my books to him for the men. His response to me was, send thirty of them. I was able to do that by sending them through Chaplain L. who made sure they were given to Graham's Chaplain.

My son brought powerful Spirit filled worship to the guys that day and it certainly plowed hearts to receive the teachings. Though we did our best to follow our intended purpose for the one-day seminar, we eventually surrendered to the leading of the Holy Spirit.

Our team left prison that day excited about our experience with not only the prisoners, but with the chaplain. We were hopeful it would not be long before we were given another opportunity to return. I had already learned that the wheels did not turn faster just because I was anxious to see if there was more God had for me with prison ministry. I continued to trust that He would open another door to take the team in. I knew I needed to wait and be ready to surrender to wherever He was taking me. I would soon be challenged to take the next step in prison ministry that I was not anticipating.

I eventually received a call from Nathan asking me to apply to be badged with the Safford Prisons. It brought to my remembrance the conversation I once had with Nathan over the past year concerning the restrictions that are placed on volunteers who decide to be badged. No longer would we be allowed to personally communicate with the prisoners once we leave the prison. The personal contact I was able to have with the Douglas Prisoners as a volunteer, was not going to happen once I was badged. I chose to move forward with the badging process and was e-mailed the forms and requirements that I needed to start working on.

It was certainly a little intimidating and overwhelming when I realized what was involved in the process. I sat at my computer printing out page after page of requirements that had to be filled out which included a ten-page background check, and a paper on my criminal history. I was confident I had no criminal history other than perhaps a forgotten speeding ticket that might show up. I knew every page would be scrutinized by prison security.

I managed to submit all the necessary paperwork and waited to hear what I needed to do next. I was required to watch and be tested on several videos pertaining to important details for volunteers. I eventually received a call from the head chaplain to return to be fingerprinted. Once my fingerprints and security information were cleared, I was called to come pick up my badge. I had no idea where this badge was going to take me and if this was a part of the unforgettable journey I was being taken on.

Bob and I drove to the Safford Prison not certain what I should feel over the opportunity to finally receive my badge after a month-long process. I wish I had given some thought that day beyond my excitement as to what the negative connotations would be that would eventually accompany this badge I held in my hand. It was not until I fell in love with the prisoners that I would feel the effect of my limitations.

We pulled up to the prison yard gate and announced that we were there to meet Chaplain L. to pick up my badge. I knew we could expect to be asked the same security questions each time we entered the yard gate before we were permitted to enter. No one gets past the yard gate without having prior authorization. If it happens to be visitation day, the families are required to pull into an area that will be searched for contraband. Chaplain L. was expecting us when we pulled up to

Control and showed us where we needed to park. The Safford Complex holds two separate prison units that are housed on the same property that are a short distance from each other. Chaplain L. believed in walking everywhere even though you could drive to where we were going. I am certain he was preparing us for walking the distance between any security gate and the prison chapels we would be ministering in.

We followed the Chaplain to the building where I would be picking up my badge. I do not remember looking at the badge while walking back to our car. I suppose I did not want to appear overly excited, but I am sure I was that day. When I started to get into the car the chaplain looked at me and said several times "Janene, you can go to Fort Grant tonight and start ministering." Not sure if he was serious as he knew I would have to go it alone. Bob would not be allowed to go with me as he was still going through the badging process. No longer could you volunteer in the Safford prisons unless you were first badged.

With a smile on my face I turned and looked at the chaplain and said, "I don't think so!" I knew Bob had the gift to touch these prisoners with his preaching and I was not prepared on the spot to preach to them. I had already been in one of the prisons in Safford with a team and was not afraid to walk among the prisoners alone. I had never been to Fort Grant's Prison and was clueless as to what to expect or where the chapel was located. I knew it would not be long before Bob would receive a call that his badge was ready for pickup, at which time we would both be going together.

Eventually my husband Bob received his badge and we became a ministry team once again and found ourselves walking through open doors at Fort Grant, Arizona Men's Prison. We were to meet the chaplain outside of security where he handed Bob his badge and was kind enough to walk with us to the chapel, where he introduced us to the men before leaving for the day.

Chaplain L. has opened doors for us that

otherwise would not have been open. He has shown me such grace and mercy at times when I have unintentionally crossed the line for those who are badged. Not once did I take the time to consider that meeting positive needs has a limit when being a volunteer.

-5-

Fort Grant Men's Prison

NESTLED AT THE BASE of Mount Graham, sets Fort Grant Men's Prison. It was once a former United States Calvary fortification in the U.S. state of Arizona. The post is named for Ulysses S. Grant, the 18th President of the United States. Its buildings are laid out much like it was when the fort was active during the Indian uprising and Apache wars. It seemed to be a unique opportunity for Prison Fellowship's volunteers to minister here. I have come to the realization that there truly is something special about Fort Grant.

Fort Grant Men's Prison

Fort Grant Prison Ministry
April 5th, 2019

Bob and I were now both badged and anxious to start our ministry at Fort Grant. We made plans to team up with Chris and Stephnie who would be working with us. Though we all qualify with the ability to lead a team, it was somehow laid at my door. I was not certain at the time what all this would mean for me. Was I strong enough to lead with authority, and yet seasoned with grace? Would I make mistakes in the role I've accepted?" Possibly! Nevertheless, I am thankful I was given the opportunity to lead this amazing team.

Before we could start our first service, I would need to communicate with Chaplain L. concerning any available days and times the chapel would be open to us for ministry. Chaplain L. has oversight over three Safford prisons with a heart to meet the spiritual needs of all the prisoners. His responsibilities include making the chapel available for different faiths throughout the week to have meetings regardless of their beliefs. His expressed desire to us was to see at least one faith based Christian service each week be provided to the prisoners at Fort Grant.

There is one volunteer who currently travels to Fort Grant to cover the first Sunday service of every month. This leaves the rest of the month without any non-denominational meetings for the men. Though many of the prisoners are Christians, they are not allowed to hold meetings in the chapel without an outside volunteer present. Our team was determined to help the chaplain wherever we were needed.

It did not take long to receive a response back that the chapel would be available to us on Friday nights and Sunday mornings for ministry. I made a call to Chris and Stephnie to discuss what they felt they could commit to. They were already doing two Friday nights a month ministering to women at the Bisbee, Arizona Jail, as well as quarterly seminars at the Douglas, Arizona Men's Prison. After discussing our options, our team decided on two Sundays and two Fridays a month each. This would fill the need for at least one service a week at Fort Grant for the prisoners.

Chris and Stephnie were still working on their paperwork for the badging process and did not expect it to be approved for a month or so. There was no question in our hearts about Bob and I filling the need until they were available to minister with us. I contacted Chaplain L. to let him know what Sundays and Fridays we would be willing to commit to.

It was a month before our first scheduled service

at Fort Grant that I found myself struggling with what to expect. As a team leader it was my responsibility to prepare for our services. My past experiences with prison ministry called for us to bring the worship team with us. Though I loved to worship, I certainly did not have a calling to stand up and lead in front of these men. Stephnie, one person on my team that qualified was not going to be badged for a month. I continued to stress over the situation, and no matter how I painted the picture in my mind, it was not a very comforting one. Chaplain L. would continually assure me that the clerks handle everything including worship, and we need only to bring our Bibles and a message. Clerks are prisoners who are assigned to different positions where they are serving their time. They are given opportunities to work in areas they might qualified for, or are interested in. There are chapel clerks, yard clerks, kitchen clerks and numerous other jobs.

Did I trust his advice and take it to heart? Not really! I could not shake from my mind the image of me standing in front of prisoners I had never met and leading worship. I had complete confidence that there would be a message that first service. I was bringing the messenger with me. I have never known my husband not to have a message ready to deliver at a moments notice. Was it enough to calm my anxiety about worship and dispel the image in my mind? No! Whoever said, "seeing is believing," certainly had me in mind.

So many times, in life I obsess over situations that never come to pass. This was not the first time, and it certainly will not be the last you will read about. Not only did the clerks have everything in control, there was no need for a worship leader. These men could blow the roof off the chapel with their voices, and not one person needed to be up front leading them. Once again, I caused myself unnecessary stress over something that I did not need to be concerned with. Though I was excited to see how well the clerks handled the worship portion of the service, it did make me feel rather foolish over the time I spent worrying. It left me wondering if I would ever reach a place in my life where I would simply trust the Lord and let go of wanting to control everything. One can only pray and hope!

I will never forget the first time I walked into the chapel with Bob and this chaplain. I was unaware at the time that the chaplain had brought a couple of my books over to Fort Grant that I had previously sent into the Graham Unit. I had just stepped inside the door when a couple of the prisoners said "We know who you are. You are the one who wrote "Good Girl Bad Girl." Apparently, I did not need any introduction those first few moments walking into the chapel! It certainly put me at ease at a time where I was clueless as to what I was walking into.

It was only after a few Friday nights with these men that we realized we could not limit ourselves to just a few services a month, when the need was evident and the prisoners where asking for more.

When you hear people talk about being addicted to something, we understood exactly what they meant. We were now addicted to prison ministry and found ourselves in love with the "guys in orange." We decided to make a commitment right from the start to do every Friday night, and all but one Sunday a month at Fort Grant.

The excitement we feel each time we are given an opportunity to be with these men never diminishes from one service to the next. The prisoners quickly became a part of our family. I find myself in awe as I stand at the back of the chapel during services with emotions that cannot be explained in words. I am witnessing a room filled with prisoners standing and worshiping their Lord, and there is no pretense as to who they are worshiping. I wish I could take a video and show the world what it looks like when men surrender unashamedly to their God. When worship is over and Bob stands up to bring the teaching, he has an audience engaged, attentive and open to what is being taught.

Fort Grant has several gifted prisoners that lead Bible studies during the week on the yard. Though they are not permitted to use the chapel without a volunteer, this does not stop them from meeting together for spiritual growth. As volunteers we are there to teach and encourage them in the things that pertain to their Christian faith. They cannot deny the love we have for them each time we walk through those gates.

In the first nine months of 2019 that we were at Fort Grant, Bob had the privilege of baptizing seventy prisoners!! Most of the men were given a personal word from the Lord spoken through Bob. I am convinced that grown men do not sign up to be baptized unless they have truly heard from the Holy Spirit. What an honor and privilege to witness a part of what God is doing among the prisoners. We all carry memories in our life that make an impression on us. I was brought to tears one night when one of the prisoners being baptized came up out of the water covered his face and cried. What an emotional moment knowing God was assuring this man of His love at a time when he was struggling with the inability to feel anything. Baptism can be a powerful life changing experience.

When any prisoner has served his time and is ready to be released, we are given the opportunity to pray for them. I am so moved when I see the other prisoners come forward to surround their friends and brothers whom they have been housed with. We lay hands on them and release them out into the world in which they came. I will often take the time to remind them that they have a very real enemy out there that will try his best to draw them back into past addictions and problems. My encouragement to them is to remember **1 Corinthians 10:13, "No temptation has overtaken you except what is common to man; but God is faithful, who will not allow you to be tempted beyond what you are able, but with the temptation will also make the way of escape, that you may be able to bear it"**. The Lord will always make a way of escape for anyone at the point of their temptation, but they themselves **must** look for that point of escape.

Though we pray and trust that they will not be repeat offenders, I do want them to know that if they should fail, they can expect God to come looking for them if they are truly His. **John 10:28-29 "And I give them eternal life; and they shall never perish; neither shall anyone snatch them out of my hand. My Father who has given them to Me, is greater than all; and no one is able to snatch them out of my Father's hand."** For years I wondered why the Lord never gave up on me during the years I walked in sin. He reminded me this past year that when I asked Him into my life at the age of eighteen it was settled. My sin was not going to keep Him from coming after me and that is exactly what He did.

The excitement we feel for the opportunity to be with these men starts well before we get into the car to drive the ninety-seven miles to the prison. Each time we walk through the security gates we are overwhelmed with this amazing opportunity to again walk among the men we have grown to love. Once we leave the chapel and walk back through security there are always a few of the guys walking with us just wanting to have a few more moments of sharing their lives with us. It cannot get any better than that.

-6-

Our Fort Grant Experience

WHAT HAS MADE OUR MINISTRY at For Grant such a rewarding experience has been the responses we have received from the prisoners and staff. Officer Pulse, who lives at the prison complex, insists we park in front of his house next to his car and closer to security. You would have to understand the road conditions of this prison to appreciate what this means to us. We have grown to love this man, and each time he is on duty it is easy to walk up and give him a hug.

Not once have we been made to feel like we are an inconvenience to the guards by our arrival. We arrive on Sunday mornings and Friday evenings when the prisoners are scheduled to eat their meals which requires most of the guards to be near the cafeteria. When we show up for service it means one of the guards must return to security to check us in. It is not a skip and a jump back where we are waiting, and they have never made us feel like we have troubled them.

January 12, 2020, we arrived at the prison and pulled into the parking lot. Bob had not felt well that morning and realized when he stepped out of the car that he would never make the walk up the hill to the chapel. It was not a problem for me to cover the service that morning while he remained in the car. I knew the men respected me as I did them. We were planning to serve communion after worship, and I knew the Holy Spirit would lead. Thank you, John (prisoner) for bringing the meaning of communion in a powerful way that morning to us. Surely, God has gifted you. I walked away from service that day with the realization that the Spirit moves best when we ourselves are not given a time to prepare. I could not have imagined that we would arrive at the prison that morning and

Bob not feel well enough to walk the hill to the chapel.

When service was over, I stepped outside of the chapel, and Officer Dunaway was standing there. She said, "I came to sit with you." She knew Bob was not well that morning and wanted me to know she cared. Her heart was in the right place even though for some reason guards are not allowed to attend services. Instead, we both talked while walking back to security together. This spoke volumes to me about how blessed we are to be volunteers in the Safford prisons. Officer Pulse also heard Bob was not feeling well and approached me that morning offering for Bob to sit at his house. There will be many times throughout this book that you will hear the names of staff who have made our ministry as volunteers the success that it is. I only wish I could name them all.

Month after month I would sit at the back of the chapel with a longing in my heart to have a picture of what we were experiencing. I knew cameras were not allowed, and it felt like my desire would always remain unfulfilled. Each time I posted an update to family and friends I knew our words could not draw the picture of what we were experiencing. My sister would often say how she wished she could be a fly on the wall during our meetings to experience what we were able to. I would call her after each service and do my best to describe what it was like being with these guys, knowing my words were not enough.

If you have been saved for any length of time you know that God moves on behalf of our desires. He will work in circumstances to meet needs that normally seem unattainable. God knew my heart, and I believe He went to work to make the impossible happen. That is exactly what He did one Sunday morning when we stepped out of our car to start walking to security. There happened to be a fire in the mountains that day that kept Deputy Warden Hackney on the complex to oversee the situation. Fire crews would need a place to sleep during shifts. When I saw her walking to the offices, I stopped her and poured out my heart about wishing I could somehow have a picture of our services. I explained that we were traveling 2,400 miles each month and needed the help of our church and supporters. I knew if I could somehow show them through a visible picture, that it would encourage them to continue their support.

I honestly did not know what I expected to come from sharing my heart with her. I knew cameras were not allowed in prison. I sat many times wishing phones were permitted so that I could simply snap a picture. I knew that was never going to happen. This was prison! During our first baptisms I could not help yelling out to the men standing around, "Alright, whoever has a cell phone take the pictures." They all started laughing as we all knew phones would never be found on any of us.

The Deputy Warden listened and then said to me "We have camera's in prison. I'm having a meeting this week with the other wardens and will share that with them." I was so overcome with excitement that I asked her if I could give her a hug, and I did! I walked to security thinking, could this really be a possibility? We continued to cover our service that morning all the while feeling this overwhelming hope that something would come out of that encounter.

I patiently waited a couple weeks to see what the response would be and if she would allow someone to take pictures of our service. I remember the excitement I felt walking into the chapel the Sunday we had planned to baptize several of the guys. I walked up to John who worked with computers and photos for the prison and said, "I guess it is not going to happen." He looked at me with this huge smile on his face while reaching in his pocket and pulling out the camera that was given to him by one of the guards. He was able to take pictures of those being baptized including the few others I wanted taken.

It would only be a matter of waiting to see if I would be allowed to have any of the pictures that were taken that day. I was finally told that the head warden of the Safford Prisons would not permit me to have the pictures. I e-mailed Grants Deputy Warden thanking her for going beyond her responsibility and appreciated that she tried to provide me with pictures. I explained that in the beginning I had only wanted a picture of the guys from the back of the room and not their faces but thanked her for trying. It was not an hour later that she apparently went to the head warden and obtained approval for the pictures you see on the next page. I wish I could describe the emotion I felt when I received her e-mail.

To know that these men at Fort Grant have a warden who they respect and who genuinely cares about them is what makes this yard what it is. While ministering at Tonto last week a Lieutenant McCluskey mentioned that Deputy Warden Windy is one of the best deputy wardens in the state of

Arizona. I believe it! Though, I have only seen Grant's Warden twice in person, I hear many positive remarks about her from the prisoners. I feel as a volunteer ministering at Fort Grant, we are privileged to have a warden that truly has a heart for the prisoners.

Our Guys in Orange

-7-

Tonto Men's Prison

Love Broke the Chains

BY JUNE OF 2019 Chaplain L. had sent a message asking if we would consider doing a 9:00 am church service at the Tonto Men's Prison and a 1:00 pm service at Graham, the first Sunday of every month during the summer. Both prisons were located in Safford, Arizona fifty-four miles from Fort Grant. We understood why the chaplain asked if we could cover those services. Fort Grant's first Sunday service each month was already covered which would allow us to meet the need for the Tonto and

Graham prisoners. I read the message to Bob to see what his response would be as he would be the one responsible to do two additional messages. We were already doing seven services and driving eighteen hundred miles each month. I already knew what his answer would be when I ask him, as I know my husband's heart.

I contacted the chaplain letting him know we would be happy to help for as long as we were needed. Chaplain L. set up a meeting time with Bob and I to visit both prisons. This would allow us to be familiar with the location of each chapel before our first scheduled service. Unfortunately, we arrived for our meeting that day in blue jeans and were not permitted to enter either yard. Blue jeans are only allowed on Fridays if you are willing to pay a dollar. Being western minded people, we were more than happy to pay up. Trust me, it is worth it. It was not a Friday and because of that, we were not allowed in. We never gave it a thought as to what we were wearing that day. We did not consider it an official ministry day. Needless to say; we would not be visiting either prison yard that day. Though traveling to any of the prisons we minister at requires us to drive seventy-five to a hundred miles each way, we did not allow this to discourage us. I was familiar with where Graham's Chapel was located, but it would have helped to visit inside the Tonto Unit before we held a service there.

Our first Sunday at Tonto was scheduled for June 2nd, 2019. We arrived at the yard gate and showed the guard our badges while letting them know the reason we were there. I am still amazed that no matter how many times we have approached the gate into the Safford Prison Complex, we are received by guards who have such amazing attitudes. They of course are required to ask us the same security questions at the gate as they are when we enter a prison. From the start of prison ministry, we have made it a point to let staff know how much we appreciate the position they hold. We believe it is important to plant seeds of respect with those who have such a tough job to do each day. It is not uncommon for guards to have to pull double shifts, and still they manage to greet us with a smile.

Not having the opportunity to visit the Tonto Prison created a little uncertainty about what we should expect. We knew Tonto Unit held both prisoners serving life sentences, as well as some serving lesser time. We pulled into the parking lot and prepared to approach security for the first time inside this unit. When it comes to security, the requirements never vary from one prison to the next. The only difference is the access into each prison. As we approached the first gate it slides open and we step through. I immediately walk to a window outside of control where I drop both our badges in. We then wait until we hear the next security door unlock for us to enter. We step inside and know that another door will not open until the one behind us has closed.

We are about to repeat what we know is necessary for the security of the prison. We are handed back our badges with an assigned radio while waiting for the steel door to open so we can start the necessary inspection process. I am not sure I will ever get comfortable with the sound of the heavy metal doors being opened and closed at this prison. We remove any items that we know will be detected when passing through the scanner. After placing all items on a table to be inspected, we are cleared and ready to continue through several more security doors and gates where we are finally allowed to start our walk to the chapel. Prison chapels are not conveniently placed, and you can consider walking to them your daily exercise!

When we stepped out of the final gate into the yard for the first time, we were met by the chapel clerk. Clerks are prisoners who are assigned to work in different areas within the prison complex. The responsibilities they hold are no different than if they were doing the same job on the outside. We followed him to the chapel passing many of the prisoners while giving no thought to anything other than the excitement we were feeling. This would be our first visit as volunteers to this unit, and I was not certain how we would be received.

There was certainly no fear involved, and it seemed like any of the other prison yards we have ministered in. Until we walked out of the gate into the yard, we truly did not know what to expect. We knew that Tonto had only one Sunday service provided for them each month, and that we were there to add an additional one for them. The prisoners had been notified that new volunteers would be coming that morning but had no clue as to who we were or what to expect. I guess it is safe to say we were meeting each other for the very first time.

We were instructed that worship would be provided and we needed only to cover the message. Once again, I had no reason to doubt the outcome of the service that morning. I knew the man that was preaching the message and spent the last 43 years experiencing the way people responded to his anointing. There has never been room for pride in his life as he knows the anointing to preach is a gift God has given him. A gift that has opened the door for him to minister in four different countries. It would be safe to say that during the service that morning, the prisoners were making their own assessment of who we were, and if we would meet with their approval.

It is what developed after the service that spoke about how the men received us. While walking out of the chapel many of the prisoners took the time to shake our hands and thanked us for coming. We spent a few minutes outside talking with some of the prisoners when I was asked if we could provide some discipleship material for them. Bob was in a conversation with a couple other prisoners, and I knew I would need to ask him. I was not sure how we would be able to make discipleship material available to them as volunteers. We were limited as to what we could bring in. They seemed determined not to let us leave until they expressed their spiritual hunger for more teaching.

It was only a few minutes later that several of the prisoners asked if we could come every Wednesday evening to teach them. Apparently, Wednesday nights were open for the chapel to be used as the previous volunteer was not due back until late Fall. I knew what Bob's response would be as he could not say no to them. My concern was that we were already doing every Friday night and all but one Sunday service at Fort Grant and to add another night would mean we would now be driving twenty-four hundred miles a month. Refusal was not an option for us as Bob had already promised the Lord that he would walk through any door that was open to him. This seemed to be another one of those doors! We could make no promises to them as we would have to seek the chaplain's approval if the door was to be opened to us. It took only one message and one day to have Wednesdays approved by the chaplain.

It was only a month or so after we started Wednesday night services that Bob taught on baptism. There were several men that showed an interest in getting baptized, and it was clear we needed to honor their desire to follow in the footsteps of Jesus. We set the date for July 7th for baptisms, as we only have one scheduled Sunday service a month at Tonto. We left our Wednesday night discipleship class July 3rd with a list of twenty guys who signed-up to be baptized. On July 7th, we walked to the chapel prepared to baptize twenty prisoners. I will never forget stepping into the chapel that day and seeing wall to wall men in orange with their white towels over their neck waiting to be baptized. It was at that very moment that I would have done anything to paint the picture of what my eyes saw and what my heart was feeling while looking at these men prepared for baptism. I knew that not even a camera would have captured that moment. On the morning of Sunday July 7th, Bob baptized not twenty, but thirty-nine men!

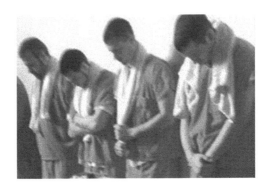

When prisoner's sign-up to be baptized they include their housing number that has been assigned to them while in prison. They have spent so many years in prison that I fear the first time they are required to sign their name after leaving prison, they will include their housing number out of habit. I understand it is a part of the system, but somehow it hurts to see them write it next to their name at times when it is not necessary. I see these guys whom I have grown to love as men, more than just a number. I can only imagine how their Creator pictures them.

-8-

Desiring More of His Presence

Blessed are they which do hunger and thirst
after righteousness: for they shall be filled.
Matt. 5:6

WE CONTINUED TO SEE a hunger and commitment among our men at Tonto. A few weeks before Christmas 2019 I knew the Lord wanted me to deliver a message to all three prisons. I have always left the preaching and teaching to Bob, as my gift is administration. I knew however that I was to deliver this message as a direct word from the Lord and not from me. The message was titled "The Walls of Jericho Must Fall." Jericho was the picture of the prison yard with unredeemed men who had yet to surrender their lives to the Lord. It was be a spiritual wall of resistance to the things of God. When Joshua was to take Jericho, his instructions were to burn the city and only bring out the **silver**, **gold**, **bronze,** and **iron** to put in the treasury of the Lord. The Holy Spirit made it clear to me that the **silver**, **gold**, **bronze,** and **iron** represented different gifts within their prison yard that God sought for Himself.

The men were further challenged with, **Matthew 18:12-14. "What do you think? If a man has a hundred sheep, and one of them goes astray, does he not leave the ninety-nine and go to the mountains to seek the one that is straying? And if he should find it, assuredly, I say to you, he rejoices more over that sheep than over the ninety-nine that did not go astray. Even so, it is not**

the will of your Father who is in heaven that one of these little ones should perish. The men in the service that day were exhorted to respond to the message. Was it possible they could be used of God to bring that one stray sheep back to the fold that the Father was looking for?

Our chapel services are always full, and it is not uncommon for there to be no empty chairs left on Wednesday nights or Sunday mornings. I knew the timing of the message had everything to do with Christmas being just 2 weeks away. We were scheduled to be at Tonto Christmas night which meant that even the unbelievers often will attend a Christmas or Easter service. I had no doubt that God knew exactly what He was doing and why it was important to give this message as a direct word from Him. My concern and last challenge to the men at Tonto was, WILL YOU MAKE ROOM for what God will do? The chapel comfortably seats about fifty-five. If they responded to the message and invited guys from the yard to the Christmas service, they would need to be prepared to make room for those who showed up. We were all praying and hoping that some on the yard would respond and attend service.

Christmas night we walked through security and headed for the chapel. We certainly had no idea what we should expect. Normally when we walk out of security we can always look to the chapel and see guys in orange standing outside waiting for service to start. We saw absolutely no one. When we turned the corner into the chapel the place was so filled with men that it was all Bob and I could do to make our way to the front where they were waiting for us! That night ninety prisoners showed up for Christmas service! There is no doubt in my mind that our guys in the discipleship class responded to the message "The Walls of Jericho Must Fall."

What an honor to spend Christmas for a few hours with our family in orange. We celebrated Christmas with worship, communion, and a

Christmas message. Our hearts were overwhelmed with what God was doing. Thank you, Lord, for trusting me to deliver Your message to the prisoners!

Stay Cool

It was on our second visit to Tonto after leaving security that we experienced something that had an impact on each of us. We had just started to make our way to the chapel when one of the prisoners listening to his music stopped turned around and said, "Thank you for coming." Our response to him was "It's an honor to be here." He continued to tell us that most people look at them so differently and would not bother coming. I often think about those words he spoke that day. We looked him in the eyes and said, "We see you and every other prisoner in here with the eyes of Jesus." He turned around and walked off as we continued to walk to the chapel.

The Shepherd in Search of His Lost Sheep

I never gave up believing that one day we would see this same prisoner walk into one of our chapel services. I am not sure I would even recognize the man we encountered that day. I hid that desire in my heart not knowing at the time that the Lord had planted it there. In the months ahead, I would understand why I could not let it go. I was soon to get my opportunity.

It was a few months later when service was over that a prisoner walks straight up to Bob and simply says "hi" and introduces himself as Stay Cool. He only spoke a few words to Bob before turning around and walking back out the chapel door. I cannot be certain, but I imagined at the time that this prisoner named Stay Cool might be the prisoner we encountered the second day into Tonto. From that night on I made it a point to pray for Stay Cool in hopes that we would see him again. I asked the men attending service if they would let Stay Cool know I was praying for him. They did not hesitate to do exactly that.

One Wednesday night during worship Stay Cool walked into the chapel. I was not sure at the time it was him, but I suspected it might be. I was standing at the back of the room and his back was facing me. He turned his head and said to me "I read your book and it was powerful." He stayed less than a minute and left the chapel while handing the clerk a piece of paper. Before worship was over the clerk handed this paper to me.

God Bless, your story was compelling and powerful, I'm so grateful for sharing with me, I even mailed it out to my daughter to read, because she too has her own father issues due to my being inside this place for so long. Finally I come home in a year →

On February 5th, 2020 Stay Cool again stopped by the chapel to give Bob some paperwork and a letter he wrote to us. He seemed to connect with Bob and felt comfortable asking him any questions he might have. I finally had the opportunity to ask him if he happened to be the guy who turned to us when we entered the Tonto yard for the second time and who thanked us for coming. He said, "Yes it was him." Until yesterday March 1st, 2020 Stay Cool had not attended a chapel service with us. What an answer to prayer when we walked into chapel that day and saw him sitting while waiting for the service to start. If a heart can be overwhelmed, that is exactly how I was feeling at that moment. We both smiled at each other and enjoyed the service.

We continue to reach out to Stay Cool who reaches out to us in return. He has shared his personal thoughts as to why he does not attend chapel and we respect them. His presence that morning in chapel service spoke volumes about how he felt about us personally. There are times Stay Cool will walk past the window to the chapel to get my attention and I am able to step outside and spend a few minutes with him while the service is still going on. The changes we see in his willingness to open his heart to us can only be credited to the Lord and prayer. I remember the first night Stay

Cool walked into the chapel and introduced himself and said one simple comment before leaving "I Believe." Could he be the one sheep on the yard that God left the other ninety-nine for in search of?

Truly God is Among Us

Worship Touching the Heart
of the Unbeliever

WHEN WE STARTED SERVICES at Tonto we were not concerned about worship. I took it to heart that worship would be provided, and it was. Carlos who has spent over twenty-three years in prison was faithfully preparing worship music each week. He would pray about the songs during the week and spent time making up music sheets to hand out. Carlos had a collection of worship CDs that he would use during the service for us to follow along with. For me, the one drawback to this method was our inability to have our hands free to worship the Lord. I found myself so focused on the paper in front of me that I lost the sense of truly being free to worship. I would often stare at the blank tv screen in front of the chapel while thinking to myself; surely there must be a way to toss the papers out and use YouTube worship videos that could be reflected on their TV.

When I walked into the chapel one evening Carlos wanted to introduce me to Diesel, Aguayo. I had seen Diesel several times in the chapel when service was over. The chapel is also the media room where prisoners can earn the right to watch a movie. Diesel was the prisoner in charge of handling the equipment. He explained to me that one of his DVD players in the chapel was a Blu-ray and should play worship videos. I was trying my best to hold in the excitement I felt at the possibility that worship videos would work. I realize with Diesel's help we could rid ourselves of the songs that were currently being put on paper if

I were able to download DVD worship music from YouTube.

I had previously bought a download program, hoping to use it when we first started at Fort Grant. Unfortunately, Fort Grant did not have a Blu-ray player. I knew I would have to be patient until the following Wednesday night to see if this would work. I am not good at practicing that particular Fruit of the Spirit. I was anxious to give it a try and I immediately went home and paid for the program again called VideoProc. I downloaded several YouTube worship songs and burned them on a blank DVD. I was beyond excited about the possibility that this could happen. I knew I would have to wait until the following Wednesday night to find out. If this worked, we were looking at the ability to bring powerful anointed worship songs to the guys.

I walked into the chapel that Wednesday with the DVD in my hand and immediately walked up and handed it to Diesel. I am watching with anticipation as he inserts it into the DVD player and to my overwhelming excitement, my prayer was answered. This was not just a small answer to the prayer of my heart for worship. It proved to be a blessing not only to me, but to the guys who no longer held paper in their hands and could focus on the words to the songs on the screen. Tonto now has hands free worship! God can answer your prayers before a sound is uttered from your lips while it is still in your heart.

The songs during worship are now visible on the tv screen allowing us the freedom to worship as we each feel the leading of the Holy Spirit. I spent the next two days in my office downloading seventy-five

YouTube worship songs. Carlos immediately turned the worship ministry over to Diesel who is now in charge of media. I assure you that worship is an important part of our services as it plows one's heart to receive the word. When we can give the prisoners a better experience during our services we step in and provide whatever approved resources we can. We are extremely thankful to Carlos for the years he provided worship for the men at Tonto. He is now able to worship freely without the responsibility of choosing and preparing music sheets. Much appreciation and thanks, Carlos!

I could not possibly stop here without telling you how Diesel's position as the media person brought him to be an ongoing part of our church services. I do not believe Diesel has ever given it a second thought about helping us. From the moment he knew we needed him he was determined to be at every Sunday and Wednesday service. When a prisoner has a certain position in prison, he is required to give an account of every piece of equipment he is responsible for. If Diesel chose not to commit to helping us, we would be back to paper worship.

I am assured when I step through those chapel doors that I will see Diesel waiting for the worship DVD I bring with me each week. I hand him the songs and he makes certain they are ready to be played in the order I request them. He is listening the entire time to the message that is being preached. He has mentioned several times he enjoys Bob's messages. One night I asked him if he had a Bible and he did not. I was able to provide him with one of our HCSB index Bibles. The Lord knew we needed Diesel's gift and it brought him to a place where he is learning about the love of Christ. I count Diesel as another part of the fabric of our lives that God is weaving in the prisons, we serve in. So grateful for you, Diesel. Just remember we are friends for life.

Having Bibles available to the prisoners is a key to seeing them grow in their relationship with the Lord. Though I have not seen a shortage of Bibles in the prison chapels, I have witnessed the problem that some prisoners have when asked to turn to specific scriptures. I watched David, one, of our prisoners at Fort Grant many times grab a Bible, locate the scripture, and hand it to any of the guys that might need help. I believe we have all felt embarrassment in church when asked to turn to a certain book and find ourselves fumbling while trying to locate where to go, hoping no one notices. I spent the rest of the service wondering how I might be able to help them. That part of who God made me to be, will not let me overlook a need. I cannot ignore the fact that I might be able to help with this situation. I know if they had Bibles with an index indented in them it would help them become familiar with the books of the Bible.

It was not long before God moved in answer to the need to make it easier for the guys to locate scripture. I had met a woman through Facebook who wanted to help buy Bibles for the prisoners. Stephanie and Joe Bekasi and their brother-in-law

John lived in Maine two-thousand miles from New Mexico. Stephanie let me know that a shipment of forty-five softcover HCSB Bibles with indexes would arrive at my house. Distance cannot hinder a prayer from being answered! It was not long before I was able to send the Bibles into Fort Grant. I should have thought at the time that when some of the prisoners started to receive their Bibles the word would quickly spread. It was not long before I was asked at every service if we had any left. Try having a prisoner look you in the face while asking if there were any more Bibles. You would have thought they were little boys in a candy store, and yet all they wanted was a special Bible for themselves. To date, new prisoners have not stopped asking for more of the index HCSB Bibles. These Bibles have been delivered to three of the prisons we minister in.

I knew I could not possibly meet their desire on my own. That is when the Datil Cowboy Church in New Mexico stepped in and sent money that allowed me to purchase fifty more Bibles. Our total of HCSB Bibles delivered to three prisons in the last ten months has exceeded over two hundred! Several guys were asking for large print Bibles making it easier for them to read. I can only imagine that some of them do not have the funds to purchase glasses that can correct their vision while in prison. All HCSB Bibles we order are large print with index capability.

One day, I asked Junior who was a friend of Stay Cool if he knew whether he had a Bible. We had only seen Stay Cool stop twice into the chapel after service. He said he thought he had some type of small book in his room that may have been a Bible. Junior agreed to take Stay Cool a Bible that I wanted him to have. It was not long before Stay Cool stopped by and handed me the following note.

> *To Mr. and Mrs. Prudler,*
> *First off, I am so, so grateful, and very appreciative beyond any words*

having received such distinguished Holy Bible. Something I will always cherish and have with me. Thank you! I sincerely do respect the impact of your unique style of spreading the Lords message abroad. Leaving your mark inside these prisons the way that you do, does not go unnoticed by me. In fact, I am deeply inspired by the way that you excite the population around me inside here. I realize that it may seem like I am not tuned-in and uninterested, but that is far from the actual case.

-10-
Prone To Make Mistakes

IN THE EXCITEMENT of becoming a volunteer, I never stopped to think about what clothes in my closet were suited for prison ministry. Bob and I were western people and everything in our closets did not seem to fit the list of do's, but plenty of the don'ts. There was not a pair of pants in my closet that would be approved. Although my tops were conservative, I usually enjoyed wearing scarves with them. For obvious reasons those would not be permitted in prison. I soon realized that prison security cared little about fashion.

I remember the first time I was scheduled to minister as a new volunteer in the Douglas Prison. I had been through Prison Fellowship's videos and instructions that included what we were not permitted to wear. Having that information did not change the fact that my closet still held nothing but jeans and tops. I lacked the funds at the time to purchase what I needed. I believed that when the Lord calls, He also equips us for that calling. Somehow that truth did not resonate with me at the time. **Roman's 8:25 "But if we hope for that we see not, then do we with patience wait for it."**

Waiting is often difficult, especially when you desperately want answers, and time seems to be running out. It is what we choose to do while we are waiting that tells a lot about who or what our trust is in. I have often failed the test only to feel ashamed when God shows Himself faithful and His provision meets my needs. It was not long until I received a message from a woman named Dusty who offered to help us. Prison ministry was close to her heart as she has a son whose been incarcerated for several years. She arranged to deposit a thousand dollars into our ministry account so that I could purchase the clothes that were appropriate and needed for volunteering in the prison. To this day when I open my closet to get ready for ministry, I am reminded about her generosity that enabled me to walk into prison for the first time. Once again, I experienced God's timely provision in answer to my needs!

This seems like a good place to encourage the body of Christ to plant seeds into the ministry that God lays on their heart. When I think about Dusty and others who have invested in our prison ministry, it is more than the clothes that sit in my closet. Every prisoner that we have been allowed to touch and fall in love with who have responded to the Lord, is to their credit as well. For the 204 prisoners we baptized this past year, including the 200 plus Bibles placed in the hands of the prisoners, to the gas that it took to drive 30,000 miles we traveled in a year, this would never have happened without their financial investment into this ministry. I do not know if it is true that the jewels in the crown we will receive in Heaven, solely represent souls that have been saved under a ministry. I would argue that jewels are earned as well from the investments we make in the lives of others that we may never see face to face. The rewards will be theirs for every life that we have been privileged to touch. Most people do not invest in prison ministry as they feel prisoners get what they deserve. Something we will challenge in another chapter.

It is important to be prepared, and at the same time know that we are prone to make mistakes at times, especially when it comes to what volunteers are not permitted to wear. When I first arrive inside Tonto's security area, I always make a bathroom stop knowing that the chapel itself has no facility. One morning when I walked out of the bathroom, I was immediately confronted by a guard that said "You won't be allowed in." Not certain why until she looked at my pants and I realized at that moment that they happened to be the color of the guards. Although I was aware that we were not permitted to wear clothes the same color of the guards, in my haste to get ready that morning it never crossed my mind that I had picked the wrong slacks to wear. I was seventy-five miles from home with no time to turn around and get back for the service. The guard was gracious enough to remind me that there was a Wal-Mart down the street. Though I wish I could honestly say that I was excited about my option, I was not! I told our team I would just wait in the car while they did the service.

Not only was I unable to enter the prison that day, I would have to leave the prison property. Waiting in the car was not an option as it was not permitted. Security sees an occupied car as the possibility that someone could be waiting to drive away with an escaped prisoner. Whenever a car is ready to leave the prison property, including ours, you will always be required to pop your trunk at the yard gate.

My heart just dropped with the knowledge that I was not permitted in. This was the first day that the

Tonto prisoners were going to see our team together in one service. We both minister to the Tonto men, but on separate days. This was our opportunity for them to see that we fully support one another. I pleaded with the guard telling her it would not happen again, but to no avail. It was decided that Bob and Chris would go on ahead and start the service while Stephnie was gracious enough to go with me to Wal-Mart to purchase a suitable pair of pants. We were both hopeful we could return while the service was still going on.

I have never been known to walk into a Wal-Mart and find a pair of pants that fit the length of my body. Though my age has caused me to shrink in height, I am 5' 9". I was desperate that morning to try on anything and moved as fast as I could to return to the prison. I rushed to the woman's section and grabbed a few pair of pants. While getting ready to try on a pair, I reached down to remove my shoes and realized at that moment that I had worn a pair of flat shoes that day with my dress pants. Something I rarely do. I thought to myself; how good are you Lord! Nothing happens by chance, and that was one of those days that I felt like the Lord was involved. If I had worn any other pair of shoes that morning, I would have walked out looking like Urkel.

I am not sure how many times Stephnie and I looked at our watches that morning hoping we would make it back to the prison with enough time to make our appearance. We arrived at the yard gate, showed them our badges, and proceeded to head to Tonto's main gate. Security was gracious enough to quickly check us through although that did not mean the security doors opened and closed any faster. We walked onto the yard that morning both of us filled with gratitude for the way God made this happen. When we arrived at the chapel and stepped into the room, we were met with cheers from the guys. I am sure that I had just experienced the fastest shopping trip I have ever made. Situations like this can happen when ministering in a prison with a strict set of rules. As frustrating as that can be at times, it is very much worth any inconvenience you may find yourself faced with.

Feeling Blessed

It has been a rewarding experience for us to minister to the men at Tonto. Our involvement as volunteers in the prisons does not focus just on those who choose to attend chapel services. We very much care about the guys on the yard that may never attend a meeting. Each time we walk through the gates of a prison we feel as though we are coming to visit our family. We have become a part of their lives, including many of the guys on the yard. I remember last summer as we passed a few guys working out that one of the prisoners said, "Hey Bob, I won't be at church tonight." Bob simply smiled and said, "Bodily exercise profits little," as we continued to the chapel. There are times when making our way to the chapel that prisoners on the yard will holler at us and say hi. It makes us feel accepted by those who will gain nothing from us. I have seen a few guys who are working out who want to acknowledge that we are there, and it speaks volumes when I watched one of the guys put his shirt on while hollering at us. Summers are so brutally hot that it is not unusual to arrive on a Wednesday night and have it register 106-108 degrees. We are happy to leave the heat and drive the seventy-five miles home where it is a bit cooler.

It is now March 6th, 2020, and the weather is starting to warm up enough so that you see more guys working out on the yard. My face lights up when I look down where the guys exercise and see little piles of rocks that represent how many times, they did push-ups or what-ever piece of equipment they are working out on.

It is the little things that we notice when walking the yard that brings a smile to our faces. For us to have the opportunity to touch the guys who are perhaps not Christians, but who recognized that we are not looking at them any different than ourselves, is what I believe ministers to them. Bob's gift of speaking in Spanish blesses me when he stops and takes the time to talk with a few men who might be standing outside the chapel that do not speak English well.

When we leave on Wednesday nights in the summer, we often see a few guys sitting on the sidewalk leaning against the enclosed fence while looking at the stars. Tonto Men's Prison is surrounded by mountains and offers anyone there some of the most spectacular sunset views. I try to imagine that perhaps they are thinking about their Creator at a time when they will no longer view these mountains from the confines of the prison walls.

We are so thankful for Tonto's open door to us. Prisoners can usually only hold down a specific job for two years before having to apply for something different. The clerk, who has been our chapel clerk since we started has gone out of his way to support us. When it was evident that Wednesday night's previous volunteer was due to come back, the clerk would have none of it. Many times, he fought hard to inform the head chaplain of reasons not to make changes. What an expression of his love for our team. Today we remain as Tonto's volunteers largely because of the clerk and the love the prisoners have for us.

When we were leaving the prison one night making our way back through security, Omar told Bob he was going to ask permission to cut his hair. Omar's job in prison is that of a barber. We knew he was serious but gave no further thought to him desiring to do that. This was a prison and we certainly did not think anything would come of it. The following Wednesday as we were walking back through security Omar say's "Bob, I got permission to cut your hair." There were two guards standing there and I looked at them and they said "Yep, the captain said he could." Up until the recent closure of the prison due to the virus, Omar has been cutting Bob's hair every three weeks. The blessing for us is to see Omar cut hair at the same time telling us how God is working in his life, and the life of his family. We are truly blessed.

The staff is incredible at all the prisons we are privileged to minister in as you have already read. One evening as we approached the chapel at Tonto one of the officers was standing outside talking with several of the prisoners who were waiting for our service to start. The officer's name was Lieutenant McCluskey, also known as Mac. In the few minutes talking with the Lieutenant you could not mistake the respect he showed for these men. Though we have been blessed by all the staff we encounter through security and on the yard, at Tonto this man has a presence about him that makes you feel thankful to be a part of the Safford Arizona Prison system.

Driving home one night from Tonto, Bob and I did our best to put into words what we were experiencing, since pictures are not allowed. We could only explain it like this: "Ministering in prison to these prisoners can only be explained by saying, "It's a glimpse of Heaven given to us on earth." We are truly blessed.

Tonto and Grahams Prison Chaplain

It is April 5th, 2020 and the prisons are closed to us volunteers due to the Covid-19 Virus. I know that most of the world has had to deal with the closures as well. Never could we imagine how difficult it would be not seeing the men we have spent the last year with while doing four services a week. Still today, July 25th, we have no idea when the prisons will once again be opened to us.

When you have grown to love these men, you have an invested interested in knowing that they are going to be fine. When we started ministry at Tonto Men's Prison in June, there was no prison chaplain at that time. Graham's Chaplain was fighting his way back to health, and recently was able to return as Tonto and Graham's chaplain. We knew that Chaplain R. had always covered the two Sunday services each week before he had health issues. With his approval, Bob and our team had been able to continue doing both Tonto and Graham's chapel services.

Then in one day, we were notified by Chaplain L. that no volunteers would be allowed into the prisons. The world has shut down, and the prison doors are temporarily closed to us. Though our team was disappointed, there was no reason to panic. We knew Graham's Chaplain would be there to cover our services, and to provide spiritual counseling to the men. To have a Christian chaplain that sees the prisoners with the eyes of Jesus as we do, has given us the confidence and peace during this time.

I continue to stay in contact with the chaplain

every week, while we wait for the door to the prisons to open back up to us. He knows how very much we miss the guys and pray for them. These are his own words he recently e-mailed to me:

> *My old heart is thrilled that "the team" is fired up for God and making a spiritual influence for the men at Tonto and Graham! I am so, so, so glad you guys are on board. I totally support your ministry in every way. Again, looking forward to meeting and knowing the team. Inmates rave how good of a preacher Cowboy Bob is! I am just an old chaplain who loves his flock. Inmates look to me as their friend, brother, mentor, and chaplain. It's all about JESUS, it's not about me."*

I wish that all prison chaplains had a heart like this chaplain. Perhaps one day in the future it will happen!

-11-

Graham Unit Men's Prison

IMAGES HAVE A WAY of planting themselves in your memory only to resurface at times when recalling the moments that have made an impact on your life. One of those images has to do with the first morning we arrived outside of the Graham Chapel. It was a warm June day and not unusual to see men standing outside waiting for the service to start. It is a sight we are familiar with when approaching any of the chapels. Though I previously had taken a team into this unit, I was not familiar with any of the men who were standing there that morning. We introduced ourselves and spent a few minutes talking while waiting for the service to start. A few minutes into our conversation, we were asked the question "Were we planning on being there every Sunday morning now?"

We knew our answer would not be what they were hoping for. They were asking for something we could not give them. We were not aware at the time that Graham had only one scheduled Sunday service provided for them each month. Our responsibility was to only cover their first Sunday service during the summer months. We were already committed to Fort Grant on Sunday mornings except for the first Sunday, which is why we were there with them that morning. When we saw their faces as they asked us that question, we knew our answer would not be what they were expecting.

It did not alleviate the heaviness my heart felt as I walked into the chapel that morning knowing we could not meet their desire for a service every week. I was not sure whether our response had the same effect on them as it did on me. I found myself unable to avoid looking around at the men I had met for the first time. Perhaps if I had not seen their faces and perceived the excitement in their voices when they asked that question, I could sit and enjoy the rest of the service. Their faces became a vision I could not seem to erase from my memory.

I have learned over the years that the Holy Spirit has a way of getting our attention in matters that are important to Him. Sometime between the opening prayer and the introductions that morning it occurred to me that there was a way we could honor their desire for Sunday services. It was one of those moments when you free your mind up and make room for the Holy Spirit to speak. No longer able to withhold my excitement at this revelation, I interrupted the service to share what I knew would bless them and bless us. Since Fort Grant's service was at 9:00 am and Graham's Sunday service was not until 1:00 pm in the afternoon, we could leave Fort Grant after their morning service and drive the fifty-four miles to Graham and cover their afternoon service.

The excitement that morning did not over-shadow the message and instead, reinforced our determination to fill their void for Sunday Services.

It would be hard to forget the room filled with men that seemed to explode with all kinds of suggestions. Their enthusiasm over the idea that they could plan a baptism seem to make the top of the list. There was no hurry on our part to drive the seventy-five miles home, so we continued to spend a few minutes visiting with them before walking back to security.

We continued to do exactly that. We started our first service on June 2nd, 2019 and scheduled our first baptism on July 7th, 2019. Every week leading up to July 7th we were told that more prisoners were being added to the list to be baptized. Not certain what to expect, we prepared ourselves as much as we could. The real preparation laid at the hands of the prisoners who were assigned to set up the tank.

We drove to the prison that afternoon and arrived in the parking lot excited knowing this was going to be our first opportunity to baptize those on the Graham Unit. We had no knowledge as to when Graham may have previously had a baptismal service. We were told that chaplains were not allowed to baptize prisoners. We followed the standard procedures going through security but before we left the last door to the yard itself one of the guards said, "They're waiting for you!" I had to smile as there was something behind the way he said that. We were about to find out.

As soon as they opened the last security door into the yard we looked towards the chapel and were speechless by what we were looking at. All we could see was a solid crowd of Orange uniforms covering the entire entrance to the chapel porch where the tank was set up! There are no words to describe what Bob and I felt as we walked the distance to the chapel! We literally had to make our way through the prisoners who were waiting to be baptized. Bob had the honor of baptizing fifty-nine prisoners that day at Graham. He had already baptized thirty-nine at the 9:00 service at Tonto. By the grace of God Bob was able to baptize nighty-eight prisoners on July 7th! He could not have accomplished that without the prisoners at Tonto and Graham that helped him lift the men out of the water. It was certainly a day to remember. Thank you, Jesus, for Your hand moving mightily!

On November 3rd, 2019, we were able to baptize sixteen additional men at Graham. Since beginning ministry at Graham, we have grown in numbers and have been moved from the chapel to the gymnasium. When we first started services at Graham, we were blessed to have Nate doing our worship and providing the music. Graham is the only prison where we minister that has an actual worship leader. Eventually the worship team grew, and Javier became a worship leader, sharing the responsibility by alternating on Sundays with the help of several gifted musicians.

On December 22nd, 2019 we celebrated a bilingual Christmas service at which Javier led worship. My relationship with the Lord has shown me that He often goes beyond our expectations in the ministry. December 22nd proved to be one of those days that we were not expecting. Walking into the gym that day we encountered a scene that neither Bob nor I could have imagined. We knew we could expect our worship leaders to be prepared to lead us in Christmas worship. What we were not expecting was some amazing pre-worship music by many of the prisoners with instruments that we normally do not see. Saved or not, they brought us worship that left us speechless and filled to overflowing with Christmas music. The added blessing for me was to see one of the prisoners' rap to the song, "Oceans."

Our Bi-lingual Christmas service that morning exceeded all our expectations. When the message was preached about the Walls of Jericho needing to fall, there was a group of men that took that message and ran with it. They set plans in motion to do their part to walk the yard while praying and reaching out to those that would listen. They met as a group of men who were determined to respond to the message, and they did!

One of the last scriptures I spoke that morning as a direct word from the Lord was found in Ezekiel 3:16-21. *"Now it came to pass at the end of seven days that the word of the Lord came to me, saying, "Son of man, I have made you a watchman for the house of Israel;* **therefore hear a word from My mouth, and give them warning from Me:** *When I say to the wicked, 'You shall surely die,' and you give him no warning, nor speak to warn the wicked from his wicked way, to save his life, that same wicked man shall die in his iniquity;* **but his blood I will require at your hand.** *Yet, if you warn the wicked, and he does not turn from his wickedness, nor from his wicked way, he shall die in his iniquity; but you have delivered your soul. "Again, when a righteous man turns from his righteousness and commits iniquity, and I lay a stumbling block before him, he shall die; because you did not give him warning, he shall die in his sin, and his righteousness which he has done shall not be remembered;* **but his blood I will require at your** *hand. Nevertheless, if you warn the righteous man that the righteous should not sin, and he does not sin, he shall surely live because he took warning; also, you will have delivered your soul."*

Many prisoners took to heart the message given to them by the Lord that morning. Our Christmas service doubled in attendance and brought ninety prisoners to hear the message. It was only a few weeks after Christmas that the same group of men asked Bob to have a special service to anoint them to continue to touch their yard. We brought anointing oil that morning and anointed five to seven men who came forward. Once again when the Spirit decides to move, He will not ask your permission. The men who received prayer to be anointed that morning immediately turned and began to pray over their brothers. No one seemed to be in a hurry as we watched men waiting to be prayed for. I can only describe what happened that morning as supernatural.

There is a hunger among these men that we have

never experienced as pastors in our thirty-eight years of ministry. Both Bob and I feel as though we are experiencing the greatest time of our lives with the opportunity to be with these God seeking men. It has become both a humbling and honoring opportunity given to us in the last days of our ministry. Psalms ninety-two has given us the encouragement that even in our seventies, God is able to still use us to touch lives. We hope to continue to be a part of Prison Fellowship until the Lord calls us home.

In all the previous years of my ministry I had never felt the freedom to be exactly who God made me to be. I spent years wanting what I saw in others who seemed to have a gift for ministering that seemed so natural. For years, the ministry seemed to have an element of fear attached to it for me. I was just not as comfortable as I would have liked. I remember well the day it dawned on me that I only needed to be what God made me to be and nothing more. He placed gifts in me that He knew I would need to fulfill His ordain purpose for my life.

I stand before all our guys in orange today knowing that like them, I am one who understands what it is to be forgiven of my past. We choose to look at each prisoner through the eyes of Jesus. We will never ask why they are in prison, and neither do we care or need to know. We are there to teach them that they can experience freedom in Christ whether they are incarcerated for a short period of time, or perhaps are given a life sentence. Though we are required to carry a radio once we leave security and go into the yard, never have we had a reason to fear being among the men. We are a part of their family, and know they have our back.

Though I am thankful that many of the prisoners have read my book, I can honestly say that there is no room for pride in my heart. I responded to what I will always believe was an assignment from the Lord. Without the Holy Spirit "Good Girl Bad Girl, My Father's Daughter" would not exist. I honestly believed in the beginning it was written to help people discover the love of the Heavenly Father. So many times, we feel so unworthy of His love. So not true! It was this past year that I realized my story was also meant to encourage others that God can use those who are broken and bring restoration to their lives.

I am often reminded of what Jesus said to the group of scribes and pharisees who brought the woman caught in adultery before Him to be stoned. "He who is without sin should cast the first stone." Her accusers departed realizing not one of them was without sin. No need for stone throwing here in prison as we all stand guilty and in much need of a Savior. I know with a certainty that every prisoner who has read my book can understand that they are looking at two volunteers standing before them who have not lived perfect lives. Never should they feel their past would prevent them from being used of God!

-12-
Freedom Behind Bars

Now the Lord is the Spirit, and where
the Spirit is, there is freedom.
2 Corinthians 3:17

Walls, Wire and Confinement

THE PRINCIPLES AND TEACHINGS found in this chapter are not only for those who find themselves behind bars, but to each of us who are surrounded by circumstances that are a prison of a different kind. Regardless of what each of our walls currently look like, we need to learn to build a **spiritual wall** that the enemy cannot breach. The only way for us to do that is to learn from our past mistakes and use the tools and time God has given us to repair any defects in our armor. You can be assured that the enemy (Satan) will take advantage of any opportunity he can get to penetrate your wall when he recognizes an opening. It is your responsibility to strengthen your spiritual defenses and close the gaps that the enemy might use to gain access to your life.

Much of what is shared in the following pages is to encourage prisoners that God has a plan for their lives regardless of their current situation! They will learn that true freedom is not governed by the walls around them. They may have arrived at their current destination in chains, but never do those chains have to hold them back from experiencing the true freedom that can only be found in Christ.

Understanding what freedom is **not** will help us begin to put aside any excuses we might be tempted to use for why we cannot fulfill God's ordained purpose for our lives. **True freedom is NOT dependent upon our physical or outward circumstances.** The sooner you no longer see these walls and wires as your enemy but your teacher, you will find it easier to accept that God has a purpose for your life right where you are at. Do not allow your circumstances to hold you back. Let whatever situation you are in become your training ground for what God wants to do in and through you. The best prison security system in the world will not keep out the Teacher, (Jesus) who walked through walls to be with his disciples. He is willing to take any place in your life you are ready to give Him. He is not asking any of us to fulfill His purpose for our lives on our own. You are the only one who can choose to invite the greatest teacher into your circumstances. **John 13:13 "You call Me Teacher and Lord, and you say well, for *so* I am."**

Freedom in Christ is NOT a license to do whatever you want. Our freedom is to be used responsibly and for a good purpose. In this case, God's ordained purpose. Freedom is where the Spirit of the Lord **is**. As a believer you have been given the Holy Spirit's voice to help you make right choices. The moment you make a decision that is contrary to the word of God, you have created a breach in your wall.

Freedom is NOT to live the way you choose. The course of your journey has everything to do with the choices you make. Man is without excuse when it comes to making the wrong choices. We have God's word that clearly gives us guidelines in the way which we are to live.

Freedom is Not about entitlement or happiness. As soon as you realize that the world does not owe you anything, the sooner you will open yourself up to receiving only what God has for you. Can you truly experience freedom in Christ in the situation you are in? Yes! Does God have an ordained purpose for you while you wait to hear the parole board say you are free to leave? Yes! You have been given an opportunity to transform your life using the tools God has equipped you with. If you allow God to make the transformation in your life, you will be transforming the lives of your family.

Where does transformation begin in the life of a Christian? If you are a brother or sister in Christ and find yourself behind bars, you should be able to think back at a time where Jesus stepped into the circumstances of your life and said, **enough is enough**. Though you could not possibly recognize it at the time as an act of love on His part, it nevertheless brought you to the end of a destructive time in your life. If you read my book "Good Girl Bad Girl, My Father's Daughter," you know that God placed a wallet on a bus stop bench that ultimately led to my arrest and the catalyst for the beginning of my transformation.

When those handcuffs were placed on my wrists, I could not see it as the hand of God. Instead, fear and uncertainty became my companion until I heard these words spoken, "Jesus can forgive you." That was the defining moment for me when I knew my life would never be the same again. Before I answered His knock on the door of my heart, my addiction to alcohol is all I lived for. I could not possibly understand at the time of my arrest that God was at work preparing me to fulfill His plan for my life.

Since that time, I have never looked back with a desire to return to a life of destruction. **Rev. 3:20 "Behold, I stand at the door and knock. If anyone hears My voice and opens the door, I will come into him and dine with him, and he with Me."**

Though my old life no longer occupies a controlling place in my heart, it was not always so. When I first accepted Christ, I knew I was saved, but that was the extent of my knowledge as a Christian. Was it enough to keep me walking the straight and narrow? Not at all! I had no spiritual influence in my life and the world's appeal offered a picture of what I thought would satisfy me. I chose to do what people in the world do without Jesus, sin! Not once was I able to completely remove the Holy Spirit's conviction from my thoughts during the entire time that I walked away from Him. It was as though the guilt I was feeling was like a cloud overhead that never disappeared and followed me everywhere I went. Perhaps God allowed that sense of remorse to remain in my heart so I would not forget the One I had previously given my heart to. I cannot speak for those reading this book, but I was never able to feel comfortable in the act of sin without my conscience letting me know how wrong it was in the eyes of Jesus.

Perhaps many of you previously opened your heart to Jesus but soon found the worlds attraction too much to resist. Maybe you bought into the lie that what the world has to offer is the only thing that can give you the high you are looking for. Whether it is drugs, alcohol, sexual gratification or whatever your addiction looks like, you continue down that road until the high wears off and you realize that this lifestyle you were trying to maintain is destroying not only your life, but the lives of those closest to you. Whatever you were searching for in the world no longer brings you gratification. You find yourself powerless to stop the very thing that is destroying your life. You need help, and help comes from the One person in your life that refuses to let you go! Until you take the time to look back on that moment when perhaps the strong arm of the Lord caught up with you, you will not be able to recognize it as the One you once gave your heart to.

Much like the parable of the prodigal son found in **Luke 15:11-32**, many of us reach a place in our lives where what we thought we were looking for could not be found in the world. We realize we traded the Lord's gift of life for temporary pleasures and it is time for the prodigal son or daughter that we are, to return to the person who loves us unconditionally. The One who loves us too much to leave us where we are at. I can only hope that we each arrive at the place in our relationship with the Lord that the world no longer holds an attraction for us, and we hear His voice say "Come Home, My blueprint for your life looks different than yours."

If you have made the decision to rededicate your heart to the Lord, you may question if the gravity of your past sin disqualifies you in some way from the purposes God has for your life? The answer to that question is, unless you have stopped breathing, He will never be finished with the work He desires to accomplish in you. To alleviate any doubt you may have, you have only to look at the life of Paul to know how God took the man who was destroying His church to a man who changed the history of the world. A man who wrote a large part of the New Testament Bible.

So, if you think God cannot use you because of your past, think again. God met Paul on the road to Damascus and said to him in so many words "Enough is enough, Paul!" Paul at the time was breathing out murderous threats against the Lord's disciples. He was commissioned by the high priest to arrest both men and women who were followers of Christ. He stood by watching Stephen, one of Jesus' disciples, being stoned to death while consenting to his death. **Acts 22:20.** Paul's life did not look like someone God could possibly use for His greater purpose. Yet, God saw something in Paul that only the heart and eyes of Jesus could see. Many people look at our lives and often question if God could possibly use us to make a difference in the world. Like Paul, God sees something in us that we cannot see for ourselves. We simply need to surrender and say, "Here am I, Lord."

Paul's pre-conversion story may look similar to what your past looked like at one time. The question we need to ask ourselves is, what will our response be when Christ confronts us with our sin? When God spoke to Paul on that road to Damascus his response was **"Lord, what do You want me to do?"** He gives Paul just enough information to start his journey to transformation. How you respond to the Lord when you are confronted with sin is critical to what God is able to do in your life. Will you respond as Paul did with limited information as to God's plan for his life or will your response look like Adams who found it easier to blame someone else for the reason he fell to sin. Some of you blame your home environment for the choices you have made. That will never be a good enough excuse to keep you back from changing your life. God does not expect you to be who you are not, but He does want you to be all that He made you to be. Take the first step and ask the Lord, **"What do You want me to do?**

What did Paul do with his life after his Damascus experience that we can model our life after? **Philippians 3:13-14 (NKJV) Brethren, I do not count myself to have apprehended; but one thing I do, forgetting those things which are behind and reaching forward to those things which are ahead, I press toward the goal for the prize of the upward call of God in Christ Jesus.** If you are to press towards the goal God has called you to in Christ, you must decide to let go of any baggage that holds you back. It is only reasonable to assume that if you were given a sentence and incarcerated, you probably brought with you plenty of baggage that could hold you back from the God given purpose for your life. Who you were is no longer who you have to be now! Let go and leave your past behind you and live for God.

Past Mistakes, Unforgiveness, Addictions, Guilt

Could Paul have moved towards God's goal for his life if he did not first let go of his past belief system about who Jesus was? Did Paul allow his chains and incarceration to stop him from carrying out God's plan for his life? No! He never allowed his circumstances to stop the call of God on his life. No longer was Paul's authority under the religious leaders, but it was under Christ and he uses it throughout the rest of his life to preach the Gospel. **2 Timothy 2:9 "For which I suffer trouble as an evildoer, even to the point of chains, but the word of God is not chained."** The Apostle Paul was housed as a common criminal though he was bound in chains and always in the company of a guard. Sound familiar? He had favor among the guards and was respected as an Ambassador for Christ. You have the same opportunity as Paul did to gain the favor of the guards that you must submit to. Joseph was falsely accused and thrown into prison but never compromised his integrity and still found favor with the guards. Follow Paul, Joseph, and John's example and do not allow your circumstance to stop you from touching a world for Christ. Joseph told his brothers this, **"But as for you, you meant evil against me; but God meant it for good, in order to bring it about as it is this day, to save**

144

many people alive." Show the world that your circumstances cannot stop you from the work God has called you to! Be a world changer!

You can choose today to make the most of your situation and use it to further the Kingdom of God. Lead by example and do not allow those walls to stop the plan God has for you to be a vessel to effect eternity. You have a purpose that He expects you to live out whether you are living on the inside or outside of these prison walls. Use this time as your training ground for God's greater purpose in your life. **Your purpose:** You were eternally created, strategically called, shaped for His eternal purpose, designed to respond to Him with total love, trust, and obedience. He wants to be glorified in and through your life.

I realize that much of this chapter has dealt with those who are incarcerated Christians, but my prayer is that we all gain from the Holy Spirit's wisdom spoken throughout this book. Perhaps it will help keep some from making the mistakes we and others have made. To see my readers being challenged to never walk away from Jesus once they have opened their hearts to Him, is what I would hope for any of you.

-13-

Reducing Recidivism in the Prisons

ISAIAH 61:1-2 (NKJV)

• 61 "The Spirit of the
Lord GOD is upon Me,
Because *the LORD has anointed Me,*
To preach good tidings *to the poor;*
He has sent Me *to heal* the
brokenhearted,
To proclaim *liberty* to the *captives,*
And the <u>opening of the prison</u>
to those who are *bound;*

Why We Are There?
What Can You Do?

RECIDIVISM IS THE TENDENCY of a convicted criminal to reoffend.

As a Christian ministry within the prison walls, we are there to help prevent recidivism. The tendency of a convicted criminal to reoffend is high. Those that have never been incarcerated cannot fully grasp the depth of despair that overwhelms men and women who have lost their freedom. **We are there** to give them hope and teach them that through Christ they can experience freedom regardless of their past or current circumstances.

Recharge Ministries passion is to see the lives of the prisoners we minister to encouraged, strengthen, recharged, renewed, and restored so that they may walk in the fullness of all that God has for them. We believe it has never been more important for God's people to be equipped for bringing in the harvest. For many the harvest means their brothers and sisters who are housed within a prison.

What about the families of those who are incarcerated? Research will gladly supply you with articles on the effects it has on their families. Single moms trying to survive while daddy is in prison. Grandparents having to care for their grandchildren because mom is in jail. If our ministry focus is only on the prisoner with no thought as to the effect a changed life will have on the family, then we are guilty of being narrow-minded. Every transformed life brought about in prison means the potential for families to be healed and restored. Each time we arrive at the prison it is not just for the guys we have grown to love, but for their families as well.

Being with the prisoners has given us an insight as to what they are experiencing emotionally due to the choices they made that brought them to prison. I realize it is difficult for much of the world to have sympathy towards prisoners who they feel as though are only getting what they deserve. This attitude keeps the righteous from looking into the heart of the men and woman as though they can never be forgiven. This mindset from the world I can expect, but from the body of Christ there is no excuse for being so shortsighted and merely only seeing their offense. When the Lord looks at us, He sees our potential.

We are all a work in progress unless you view yourself as having arrived at perfection. Does not the Bible tell us that all have sinned and fallen short of the Glory of God? May the eyes of your understanding be opened to the way Jesus truly looks at each of these prisoners. Learn to love what Jesus loves, and self- righteousness will have no place in your life. **We are there** because we recognize that we are all in need of God's grace. **Romans 5:8 "God demonstrates His own love towards us in that while we were yet sinners, Christ died for us."** Was His blood enough for you, but not enough for the men and woman who are incarcerated?

No one knows the hour or day when the Lord will return, but what we do know is, it is forthcoming. We believe it is time to see the lost saved. **Joel 3:14 "Multitudes, multitudes in the valley of decision! For the day of the Lord is near in the valley of decision."**

Why are we as volunteers there? We know there are men and women on the prison yards that have not yet made the decision for Christ. If our valley includes the prisoners throughout the prison system, then we cannot limit our vision to just those who attend chapel services. It must include the prisoners we walk by on the yard while walking to the chapel after leaving security.

We believe God has called us to bring encouragement and equipping to those who are incarcerated. We do this through dynamic worship and the preaching of the word. The greatest gift we can bring them is the love of Christ revealed through us. *We are there* for the families as much as we are for the prisoners. We may never set eyes on their family members, but that does not mean we do not have an invested interest in them. We have been given an opportunity through our conversations with the prisoners to get to know many of their families without personally meeting them face to face.

What you can do to help prevent recidivism among the prisoners?

Volunteers Needed:

The love we are experiencing is something we wish we could pass on. Becoming a volunteer allows you to see the prisoners in ways the world does not. You will grow to love them as they grow to love you. When you walk into chapel and you are handed a miniature pulpit that a prisoner made you out of a bar of soap, or a replica of a cowboy hat for Cowboy Bob made out of toothpaste and toilet paper, you know that they are expressing their love for you. It becomes more of a sacrifice for them when you know that they are only given one bar a soap a week and one roll of toilet paper. You will never give out more love than you get back from the prisoners. If you have love in your heart, you have the beginning of what it takes to be a volunteer.

Be a voice:

You can help prevent recidivism as volunteers by sharing your experiences with the prisoners, to those of your family and friends. Understand that those on the outside must use their imaginations when we are given an opportunity to express in words what God is doing through our ministries in the prisons. Communication is vital if we are to change the way many on the outside see those who are incarcerated. Our voices speaking out is all we have, to connect words with pictures. We have the potential to change the hearts of those who see prisoners as undesirable, for those who can become viable assets to any community if given a chance.

Write a prisoner:
https:www.writetoprisoner.com

Having someone on the outside world can foster a positive and healthy attitude for the prisoners. Those who will take the time to write and support a prisoner have given them much needed hope that they would otherwise not have. It will help them believe that people truly care about them despite the choices they have made in the past. Letter writing a prisoner is one key that can help them succeed after their release.

Inspire others:

Inspire others to get involved. Until you put yourself in the presence of these prisoners you will have a difficult time seeing them not as criminals, but as human beings deserving of another chance at life. As volunteers we are not there to judge them. We do not ask why they are in prison. We truly do see them with the eyes of Jesus.

Love the prisoners as much as Jesus loves them:

Matthew 25:36-40: "I was naked, and you clothed Me; I was sick, and you visited Me; **I was in prison and you came to Me.**" Then the righteous will answer Him saying "Lord, when did we see You hungry and feed You, or thirsty and give You drink? When did we see You a stranger and take You in, or naked and clothe You? Or when did we see You sick, or in prison, and come to You?" And the King will answer and say to them, "**Assuredly, I** say to you, in as much as you did it to one of the least of these My brethren, you did it to Me."

Become a part of Prison Fellowship:

Prison Fellowship is a ministry started by Chuck Colson and can be your open door into becoming a volunteer. Prison Fellowships involvement in prison ministry has done so much in preparing prisoners to return to life on the outside. They offer many volunteer opportunities and programs within the prison, as well as helping prisoners once they are released. You have only to go to their website to begin the process.

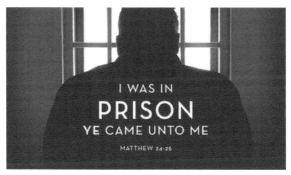

https://www.prisonfellowship.org

-14-
God Hears Our Prayers

"But the LORD said to Samuel, 'Do not look at his appearance or at his physical stature, because I have refused him. For the LORD does not see as man sees; for man looks at the outward appearance, but the LORD looks at the heart.'"

I Samuel 16:7

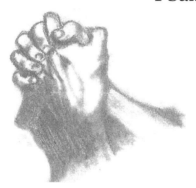

A look into their hearts

YOU WILL BE GIVEN an opportunity to experience the depth of emotions these men must live with every day. My only desire in allowing you to see into the heart of these men through their words, is to help you realize they are more than just criminals. They are sons, fathers, brothers, and uncles. These men that the world so harshly judge, have experienced forgiveness and have committed their life to Christ. This does not mean that all will succeed at preventing a return to prison. What it does mean is this, God will never abandon them if they are truly His.

What is so amazing about these prayers is their desire to see their families come to know the Jesus they know. They have experienced peace in their lives and want the same for their families. This in no way removes daily challenges for them. It does mean, they do not have to face them alone.

I want to clarify that the following prayers and testimonies were written by the prisoners. For that reason, I chose not to make grammar corrections. There were times in the reading that I have had to decipher some of their words. I have done my best to express their hearts.

❤ Please Pray for my family that God shows Himself to them so that they may be saved. If you can please pray for direction for me that the Lord will use me to reveal Himself to my mom and that she gets well. She is sick with congestive heart and liver failure. Pray for my sister who is a new convert. Thank you.

❤ I would like prayer for my mother and sister. My mom is going through a battle with cancer and is doing chemo. I know she is in God's hands. Pray for her quick recovery. My sister is living like the world on the streets and has been for quite a long time. Pray for her release from a life of drugs. I know she wants help and needs help. I believe Jesus will free her from her addiction of drugs. God bless you two.

❤ I would like you to keep me in your prayers since I am getting released. I would like to strengthen my relationship with the Lord and grow stronger outside these prison gates. Pray I stay on the righteous path and not lose my way so that I can influence my family to follow the path that the Lord wants me to walk on. Pray that I stay away from my former life and keep me from sin. Thank you. Amen.

♥ Please keep me in your prayers that I stay strong in the Lord and that I do not lose the faith. The devil has been trying to attack me hard. I would also like prayer for my mother-in-law to be approved to visit me and bring my sons. May God bless you and your family. I will also keep both of you in my prayers.

♥ Pray for my mom who is dying. I just want her to make it ninety-eight more days until I come home. Pray for my dad that he makes it through the times that he is facing, and that God will make him stronger. *(This is the kind of prayer that breaks my heart. If pictures could become a reality, mine would show a son home with his arms wrapped around his mom.)*

💜 Special prayer for my entire family that we will be reunited upon my release. Prayers and blessings go to my son's sister, nephew, and wife. May you help free them from their addiction. Amen.

💜 I would like prayer for all that are still lost in the world. I know that God will take away the drug addiction from my sister so she can be a mom to her kids and start living for Jesus. I know He will do that in due time. Praise God.

💜 Help me to do better and to go home to my family soon to help my dad with his cancer. Please watch over my kids. Keep them safe.

💜 My prayer request is that the Lord will bless me with reconciliation with my loved ones. Amen

♥ Prayer for my family and kids that I can please hear from them and that everything is good. Pray that I get through all of this and get out early to help them. Thank you. *(Visits, letters, and phone communication all must go through a process to be approved. The waiting to hear from a family member can be very emotional even on the toughest of men. Committing a crime that puts you behind bars does not strip you of your emotions. Ministering in the prisons has allowed me to see the many struggles the prisoners face when dealing with their concerns for family.)*

♥ Thank you, Brother Bob, and Sister Janene for always coming and taking time out of your busy lives to share the word with us. Words cannot describe how thankful I am to you guys. I love you guys. Can you please keep my wife and family in your prayers?

♥ Brother Bob and Janene, thank you for everything. I ask you to pray for my son. I am going to ask his mom if she can let him come visit me. I have not seen him since 2016. Thank you. I also want prayer for my sister who has not found Jesus all the way yet and I want her to know what it feels like to be saved. (*These men attend chapel services and hear what we believe are life changing messages. For many of them they desire to be given another opportunity to be good fathers to their children. Can you hear his heart longing for an opportunity to be a part of his son's life?*)

♥ My dear Lord, I understand that I have not been the best child and I would like to ask you to please help me become a better man as each day goes by. I surrender every detail of my life. I leave it in Your hands. May Your will be done in me. In Jesus name I pray. Amen.

♥ My prayer is that Isaiah 33:22 be true in my life. That I be home and be a blessing to all my loved ones as I continue to seek our Lord and King. Amen *("For the Lord is our judge, lawgiver, and King who will save us.)*

♥ I would like to pray for my family in California as well as in Arizona. Pray for my daughter to ask her mom to open-up her heart and let my daughter write me. Thank you.

♥ I would like you to pray for my family and friends to open their heart and minds to the Father that I love and who I know loves us. I am thankful to be a part of His family and Him continuing to work in my life showing me His undying love. Thank you, Lord for allowing me and my little girl to be together after fifteen years. Open her heart to love and accept Jesus as Lord and Savior. Open my heart for the Holy Spirit to flow through me to do His will not mine. I love you Jesus.

♥ Heavenly Father I want to say thank you for this life you blessed me with. Thank you for sending your messengers to preach Your word. I love you. In Jesus name I pray. Amen.

♥ Lord, I ask that you bring my daughter to see me and that you instill in her mother's heart to let her come. Also, for my wife that you may bless her with work and good health, and peace of mind.

♥ I pray for my adopted son. He is very hyper and disobedient to his mother, my girlfriend. He is developing slowly in speech also. Please pray for his speech and for an obedient spirit towards his mother. I want to know the Lord more and hear his voice. I need understanding so I can be more effective.

💗 Heavenly Father please bless my mother and her husband as well as my grandma and little brother. Keep them all safe and healthy. I love You Jesus and appreciate what you do for all Christians.

💗 I R.M. would like to pray that my parole office approves my mom's new address so I can shine light and bring my family to Christ.

💗 My Lord praise You. I would like to ask that you bring peace upon the Tonto Unit. Please bless every brother on this yard. Please help me hear Your voice and feel Your presence. Please give me a willing and obedient heart. In Jesus Christ name I pray. Bless you. Amen.

💗 Brother Bob and Sister Janene, I want to please ask that you would lift all my family in prayer. For my brothers, sisters, and kids' health, and that He may do His will in their lives and take full control of it. Thank you and may God Bless you and your family.

♥ My Lord almighty, I give you thanks for always giving me all that I do not deserve and for reminding me of how unworthy I am to truly deserve your love. Thanks always and forever. In Christ Jesus name. Amen.

♥ Brother Bob and Janene, thank you for everything. If you can keep me and my family in your prayers and keep us safe from our enemies, we all have and bless us with His love. Pray that we all stay together on this yard. God bless you and your family.

♥ I would like to thank You Father above all for all that You are, and all that you have done. I thank you for sending Bob and Janene to us here in this place. I pray in the name of Your Son Jesus Christ for Your healing power to reach out to my mother and remove the pain that she lives with every day. Thank You Father for hearing my pleas to You. Amen.

💜 Hi, my mother had two strokes and now has a pacemaker. I would love for you guys to pray for her recovery. Her name is M. T. I love this lady more than my own life. I thank you. I am not a real hard believer, but I love Jesus. I know that I do. I am just blind on the Bible. Much love and respect.

💜 Please pray for my family and my little boy to be strong, happy, and ok in every way. His name is little M. and for my mother to be ok until I get out to see her saved.

💜 Special prayer for me and my entire family upon my release. For extra blessings to go to my son's sister, nephew, and wife. May You free them from their addiction. Amen.

❤ Bob and Janene, I love you guys so much. I ask that the love of God flows in my life and that I show it, speak it, and share it. I know I have a calling on my life. I just want God's love.

❤ I would like for you to pray for my mother who is on her death bed. That is what my sister said. If possible, pray for a miracle and heal my mom so she could see me again.

❤ I would like to pray for you both for blessing us weekly with your sermons. I would like you to pray for my wife and my newborn son and two beautiful daughters. Please ask God to lay His loving hands of protection on them and me until I get Home. Thank you and God bless you.

❤ Bob and Janene, I would like to ask both of you for your prayers for my daughter that's thirteen-years old. She is going through a lot

right now and is lost doing drugs. I would
really appreciate it very much. God Bless.

-15-
No Testimony
Without a Test

"These are our testimonies; that God
hath given to us eternal life, and
this life is in His Son."
1 John 5:11

THE MEN YOU WILL READ ABOUT have written their testimonies to acknowledge that God has been the source of their transformed lives. When any of us recognize that we are powerless to change what needs to be changed, we surrender to the only one who can help us. These men will face many tests before they stand on the other side of those bars and razor wire knowing they cannot face it alone. Sharing their testimony is necessary for their growth. All the mistakes the heroes of the Bible made are public record for all time. I trust the testimonies you will read will encourage you to see what the Lord can do with a surrendered heart.

The question is, can we have a testimony without a test? I do not believe so. If you are like these men and have faced situations in your life and managed to come through victoriously, you have a testimony to share. If you are currently facing a test in your life you have only to call on the Lord to see you through.

Meet Zack:

Article by John W. Kennedy

Zack's mom and grandma. *Article used with their blessings*. Article written by John W. Kennedy

Zarkary Chase Howard excelled as a student while growing up, played as a starter for three years on the varsity basketball team, and stayed involved in youth group at Buckeye First Assembly where His father is the lead pastor. Gifted with a broad vocal range, Zakary led worship at the church. Accepting

171

a district youth ministry forty-day challenge as teenagers, Zakary and his brother, Nicholas, carried their Bibles wherever they went, including school.

After graduating from high school, Zak headed off to **Southwestern Assemblies of God University**, the Assemblies of God school in Waxahachie, Texas, where his dad graduated. But Zak opted not to return for his sophomore year in the fall of 2013. Back home over the summer, Keith and his wife, Stefanie, noticed a change in Zak's behavior. Slowly and progressively he became more distant. We knew he was hurting, but he would not talk to us about anything," Stefanie says. Without his parents' blessing, Zak moved away from the family home into an apartment with friends in February 2014. Zak even got a tattoo on his neck with large letters of YWF signifying his new life philosophy of "young, wild, and free." Contrary to his upbringing, Zak liberally sampled lifestyle choices that included drinking alcohol, smoking marijuana, and trying other drugs of various kinds.

When Zak asked to return home ten months after moving out, his parents heartily agreed provided he adhere to house rules, which included attending church Sunday mornings and abstaining from drugs. Only later did Keith learn that Zak sneaked out nightly to smoke marijuana. "He made horrible choices to keep using pot," Keith laments.

THE WORST DECISION

The pretense came to a crashing halt following the events of April 28, 2015. The unemployed twenty-one-year-old Zak agreed to accompany an acquaintance, Richard Anthony Burns, to make a drug delivery in the hopes of scoring some free weed. Their relationship revolved around one activity: smoking pot. But when the third party, 18-year old Matthew Christensen, drove up to an undeveloped lot behind an elementary school, Burns pulled a 22-caliber rifle and shot Christensen seven times.

Zak and Burns stole Christensen's car and fled the scene. "I was in a state of shock," Zak tells *AG*

News. "After seeing someone shot in front of me, I was in fear of my own life at this point." Early on the morning of April 29, Zak crawled through his bedroom window. A few hours later, Keith read his morning devotions, focusing on Deuteronomy 3:22: "Do not be afraid of them; the LORD your God himself will fight for you." Little did Keith know how providential that verse would become.

Throughout the next couple of days, Zak grappled with whether to reveal the horrific ordeal to his parents. He kept silent. "I truly did want to contact authorities," Zak recalls. "But I wondered if I would put my own family at risk. I was stuck. I was numb."

The evening of April 30, Buckeye First Assembly took a lead role in a 22-church citywide evangelistic service, emceed by Keith. Zak and Nic, then 18, both attended the event. Just before ten, Keith pulled into the home driveway. A dozen officers with the Local Special Weapons and Tactics team surrounded the vehicle, holding assault rifles and hollering orders not to move. As Nic exited, Swat officers pinned him to the ground, but Zak yelled, "It's not him; I'm the one you want."

In jail early the next morning on May 1st, Zak rededicated his life to the Lord. For the next 563 days, Keith and Stefanie could not have physical contact with their older son. The murder turned out to be a high-profile media case.

"Part of me died that night recalls Keith," who has been a credentialed minister since 1988. "That first week I told the Lord I did not want to be a pastor anymore. There would be mornings I would wake up with almost a sick feeling when I remembered what our new 'normal' was," Stefanie remembers. "There was also a numbness. God's strength was my only hope."

Even though Zakary did not conspire to commit the murder and did not touch the trigger, prosecutors argued his complicity could result in a first-degree murder conviction — which potentially carried the death penalty. In a plea bargain, Zakary confessed to second-degree murder. His eighteen-year sentence includes no possibility of early release. Burns, the triggerman, is behind bars for twenty-five years after pleading guilty to second-degree murder.

Unlike many inmates, Zak exudes gratitude, contentment, and gladness. He conducts a Bible study in the prison yard and regularly counsels other convicts in his pod. While incarcerated, Zak has led 17 other inmates to salvation in Jesus, everyone from a Mexican gang leader to a white supremacist tattooed with images of swastikas and Adolf Hitler. Zak has no intention of removing his own prominent tattoos. "God uses them now to give me access and credibility to the people I minister to in here," Zak says.

Meet L

Bob and Janene,

I just want to thank both of you for your time, and love that you show us. I know that God strengthens you every time you come and blesses you in other ways. I just wanted to say thank you and touch base on this new life I am experiencing. My short testimony is I came to Christ about six years ago when darkness was closing in on me. I had everything in the free world; cars, trucks, wife, and kids except the most important thing – Jesus.

I worked for an insurance company and I contracted several jobs a month setting tile. My family are hard working with morality and values, yet I was more drawn to making bad choices. I was convicted of transporting narcotics and was given an eight-year sentence. In hindsight I am thankful now for God's mercy on me. This term I am serving is doing me a justice because my heart turned towards God. Even this is working toward the good because I love God.

I have a purpose in life and an important responsibility. God met me in my darkest hour, forgave me and saved me and started this amazing work on me.

Lefty has served his time and is now a free man.

Meet J

I was born December 13th, 1975 in Arizona. My parents divorced when I was young. I have one sister that is four years older. We were both raised by our mother that did the best she could. She worked and put herself through school which meant she was gone day and night. I became angry and defiant from a young age. At about the age of ten I started smoking cigarettes and weed. I would light fires in the alley. All red flags that my life was not headed in a positive direction. I became more rebellious and troubled. I started stealing things out of garages and cars by the time I was fourteen. I would hang around my sister and her friends who were all older. I would do things to try and impress them. I would steal alcohol for them and so on. By the time I was sixteen I used meth daily. I still smoked weed and cigarettes. I would steal anything that was or was not bolted down to support my habit.

I had a daughter at the age of 18 and a son at 19. Both from the same mother. I was around but I was not much of a father. I caught my first major case shortly after my son's birth. I was nineteen years old. The charge was aggravated assault on a police officer with a gun. My sentence was four years.

When I came to prison, I did nothing to better myself. I became worse. I got involved with a white prison gang. When I got out, I was much worse than when I came in. I was more violent. Now I was not just burglarizing everyone. I was robbing as well. I had become the worst of the worst. I was completely rotten. I spent the next twenty years coming in and out of prison. The longest of my sentences was ten years. I had come to terms with this is who I am, and I am going to die in prison. I did not necessarily want to be this way, but I have never been able to change. I have never been able to stay out of prison for more than months at a time.

My mother is a Christian. I remember one time she asked me to read the book of Genesis. I read a couple chapters, got frustrated and threw that Bible aside. That was at least ten years ago. I had one friend that was just as bad rotten as me and he was able to change his life through God. I believed there was a God, but that just was not going to happen for me. I had all but given up on life. I used drugs in and out of prison my entire life. I lied, cheated, used, and abused. I was a godless, broken and a defeated man now serving my fifth prison sentence.

I started going to narcotics anonymous meetings because I had lost my visitation because of a dirty UA. While out on the yard one day with a friend from my group, we were working on NA stuff and he asked me if I wanted to pray. I said I would. We sat there in silence for a moment and he said, "Go ahead". I said, "Oh no, you do it. I've never done that before." He said, "Okay" I bowed my head and we prayed. I felt good and I told him, I would do it next time.

I came back to my cell and laid down on my bed. I started to pray on my own. I started feeling an overwhelming sensation in my chest and my heart was able to beat for the first time. I could actually feel God loving me. There was a lot of tears and emotions. My life changed in the blink of an eye. I knew what was happening. It could have been nothing else and I wanted more.

I became a new man from that very moment. I am living a "high" better than any drug I have ever done. I am hungry for God. I read my Bible every day. I do not use drugs. I do not lie, I do not cheat, and I do not steal. I live for God. My life has gotten better in every way. I am happy. I have better relationships with my family. I was not looking for God, but he came into my life for a reason. God has big plans for me. I do not know what they are, but it is something big.

God came into my life on July 1st, 2019. I was baptized by Cowboy Bob on July 7th, 2019. I quit smoking July 10th, 2019. My life gets better every day. God has put good people around me to teach me the Word and help me with my studies. I can attend church services. I see Cowboy Bob and Janene every week. I am so grateful for the message they bring into the prison. I am grateful for God. I love You God and I promise to always follow Your guidance. I am forever your faithful servant.

Amen (J)

Meet C

Have you ever wondered why people praise God? What motivates a human to Praise God? Many people may sing, but not all singers are praising God. Praise comes forth deep from a soul alive with gratitude to the All Powerful, All Knowing, Ever Present God Creator. Worship is when such a soul moved by God breaks forth in adoration.

My story is a sad one that shines into a manifestation of God's ever-present mercy. It is for the following testimony that I praise God with all my being. For great is His mercy toward me. At twenty-one years old I was born-again, greatly was my life touched by God. I spent my first five years as a baby Christian in prison. At twenty-six years old my life freshly out of prison was not ready to face all that awaited me. Early on, numerous pastors took to me because of my zeal for God. Sad to say, most pastors I had met were lukewarm. Few seemed to have a real love for God as, they seemed to love people. God seemed to play second place in life to them. I was a young Christian and I did not know better.

I had been saved from a depth of serving Satan, the world, and the flesh to a high degree. You could say though saved I was a jacked up Christian and did not know better. Few pastors seemed to know how to fight Satan. Most served Satan by default in not serving God with every part of their being, their spirit, soul, and body.

Today I am fifty-two years old and have spent the last twenty-two years of my life in prison. About twenty-two years ago I was in a tragic automobile crash that killed eight people in the vehicle that I wrecked into. At that moment I was a backslid Christian. My life was worthless to so many people but not to God.

Prior to that car crash I had gone to see a pastor I knew for help. He turned me away because he had visitors and had to go out to eat after night church. Not even half a mile from that church, that car crash took place. A car crash that killed eight people and barely left me alive, how I do not know.

This I do know, what Psalms 86:12-13 tells us in the KJV, *"I will praise thee, O Lord my God with all my heart: and I will glorify thy name for evermore. For great is thy mercy toward me: and thou have delivered my soul from the lowest hell."* Eight people died twenty-two years ago in the horrible car crash where God spared my life.

I have run into far too many lukewarm Christians that cannot help prisoners. That is why I honestly thank God for the Prudlers. They have been a true blessing to our prison unit. They are needed to further the movement of God in these times that we are in. Thank you so much God. **His Servant C,** In Christ Jesus.

C has been Tonto's worship leader. It is evident that C spent much of those 22 years leaning on the Lord and studying His word.

Meet S

S was one of the fifty-nine prisoners baptized one day at Graham.

I am currently serving a twenty-one-year prison sentence. I am getting released in November of 2020. Throughout all these years I have been put up against multiple challenges and Jesus was there with me before I knew Him. Thank you, Jesus. This short testimony is to give God all the glory and tell you, He is the way, the truth, and the life, and the only God who defeated death and is still alive. He brought me back from the dead spiritually and the transformation He has done and continues to do day in and day out in my life, is amazing grace.

In 2014 my mother fell into an 8½-month coma after a failed liver transplant. At the same time, I was lost in addiction and prison politics. The yoke was too heavy to carry, and I had hit rock bottom and the only place I could cry out to was, our Lord and Savior Jesus Christ. On August 27, 2014 I gave my life to Jesus. Notice I said my life not my heart. It was not until July 14th, 2018 that I gave my whole heart and surrendered my life to his will and embraced my identity as a child of God! Amen! A miracle happened that day after asking Jesus to reveal that He was with me. I experienced a supernatural encounter with the Holy Spirit. Praise the Lord! He showed up and now my faith is unshakable. I now have an intimate relationship with the one and only True God Jesus Christ.

I had been baptized before and it was a life changing experience. On July 7th, 2019 I got baptized again by Pastor Bob Prudler to recommit my life to Jesus and I asked Him to elevate my spiritual maturity that day. That day was an anointed and forever memorable day because a miracle happened, He showed up. The Holy Spirit and His presence were felt that day and He let the church know His dominion is here on Graham Unit. All I can say is, Jesus is amazing, powerful and His love and faithfulness is unfathomable. He has a plan for each of His children. He revealed that I have a purpose in the Kingdom as an instrument of righteousness to bring endless broken souls to salvation. So, each morning I surrender my whole will to Him and it is no longer I that lives, it is He who lives in me. It is such a peace and joy that nothing on earth can bring.

Thank You Jesus for sending us Bob and Janene Prudler to minister and love us. I want to personally thank Bob and Janene for making such an impact here on Graham unit and we love you guys so much. I give permission to recharge Ministries to publish this testimony including my baptismal picture. Oh yeah, my mom is alive, healthy, and blessed as ever and still serving Jesus with all her heart. Glory to Jesus! I am loving every blessing and tribulation as I walk in faith as a mighty warrior and servant of the One and Only True Jesus Christ. We love You and give You Praise, honor and glory. S

-16-

Your Ministry is Found Where You Have Been Broken, Your Testimony is Found Where you have Been Restored

Meet S C

I am only "reasonably" coming to terms with my new environment being here in p.c. after being in general population for the past fifteen years straight of my seventeen years of incarceration. This is a whole different population of prisoners than what I was accustomed to. Testing my "tolerance" and "self-control" every day. It takes practice and discipline to keep my "anger" in check so I can get out of prison on schedule. My reputation is to lose my temper and over-react, (hence) the nickname "Stay Cool".

So, this explains why I stay away from crowed places or clusters of prisoners. I am not uninterested in your service or message. My distance is necessary to avoid prisoners I do not care to "socialize" with. This preventing any provocation to anger, causing any reason to jeopardize my release date of February 2021. I am known for being anti-social here.

Slowly but surely, I have been easing into the social scene because of my career choice. I am studying to be an addiction counselor who is trained to treat addicts and alcoholics once I am released from prison. I have chosen to be of service in the second half of my life leaving my mark on this world to be my legacy. Redemption for the many selfish things I have done. I want to become a contributing member of society. I am passionate about this. I have decided to start right here where I am at inside here. I must begin to be more open while becoming more social inside these places.

There is so much more to Stay Cool's journey while in prison.

He has read over three hundred and twelve books over the past seventeen years. The list of books he has read are too numerous to list. You can read Stay Cool, (Lever Brookshire) "My Purpose in Life; The Master Plan." The reason I wanted to share portions of his testimony is because you read portions of his life in Chapter 8.

Meet M

Bob and Janene

I grew up not ever knowing my real father and the father I had was over the top extreme, abusive physically and verbally as he used to say, it was for my own good. My mother who I looked to for protection was also living in bondage to fear to this man. So, growing up I could not trust or even understand the meaning of trust. I had to learn for myself.

During these years we would go to church and amazingly these pastors named Fidelia and Paul Lozano came to my aid to protect me and teach me things till this day, and I am still learning. She loved, she cared, and she taught every one of her grandchildren about Jesus. The most amazing thing I can say about them was not only did they preach the word of God, but they lived it and showed us the same.

When I had to go back home, I lived to escape and found many escape routes which led to gangs, drugs, women, jails, crime and even at the age of thirteen had my first son. At that time, I had already visited juvenile institutions and started my journey to many different facilities.

Bob and Janene, let me just say the power of prayer does much! During this journey of mine my mother and my grandmother Fifi would Pray for me 24/7. All those years I knew right from wrong and I would always hear something inside tell me not to do these things.

After many years of damaging people's lives and mine, I went to go see my grandmother Fifi. During this visit she told me, Michael it is time for me (her) to go home with Jesus and I needed to make my mind up and decide whom it is I am going to serve, "Jesus or the Devil" because something was going to happen to me.

Within a month she went home to be with Jesus and less than a year later I got stabbed in my heart and abdomen. When I got stabbed, I heard this soft voice say, "Michael ask me for forgiveness" and immediately I did and asked, "Jesus don't let me die." I was in a coma for five weeks. All my organs shut down. I was on dialysis and I could not walk. I was like a vegetable. As my mom was by my side praying and crying, she said, the Lord told her to stop crying because I was going to live. You know that 98% of people who go through the surgery I went through die and only 2% live!

You would have thought that after this incident I would have got it right! But no! After a few months of depression and low self-esteem I would go to the restroom on myself. I tried to kill myself by drinking two bottles of Captain Morgan. Once again Jesus was not allowing that to happen.

Back to what I knew which was a life of crime, I went back to prison. I just did not care any more and had no fear of what would happen to me or others. It was all about me. The funniest thing that I could say about all this is, every time I got locked up or before I went to sleep, I would read about Jesus or pray for my children.

Bob and Janene, there is so many other times where I faced death but for some reason it just could not take place. I know now that the hand of Jesus has been upon my life for a purpose. This last service we had I heard Jesus tell me that these chains that held me in bondage for many years have been broken. It is just that I keep putting them back on because I feel safe and secure when situations appear. Oh, the joy when I share Jesus with others and when I hear you guys come disciple us. I have been having this yearning desire with me that there is more than just reading the Bible.

I am not saying that it is not important but what I am saying is, I want to live for Jesus and yearn for the things He loves. I want to express Him. I want to strive for a relationship with Him in all I do. Does that make sense? I am learning so much Bob and Janene. I am forty years old and I know without a doubt that anyone besides, Jesus I will not trust or attempt to follow. I may have not had a father, but I had the most amazing protecting Father, His name is Jesus Christ. Yes, there are many things that I have experienced in life that have not been satisfying but I can say without a doubt that I am a child of God and that I am saved and have a purpose.

I ask you Bob and Janene that you pray that every step I take is only to emulate Jesus and to come close to Him every day. I pray my life reaches many and that He gives me the words to say as He opens doors. I have concluded that I have the freedom to ask what I want but He will give me what I need. I am not here to understand, but to fully trust Him.

I love you Bob and Janene. I ask that you keep us brothers in prayer that we unite in agreement. Is there any way that you guys can disciple me? Love your brother in Christ. Michael

Meet R

My name is R and I am currently serving a three and a half-year sentence. Growing up I started using drugs at an incredibly young age. I have had several attempts at trying to get sober and went to rehab twice. Anyway, I am writing part of my testimony to share what God is doing in my life. So, I will start here. I was arrested for drugs. While sitting in jail a week after my arrest, my fiancé came to see me and told me she was pregnant. Instantly my heart was shattered. How am I supposed to take care of her? Well, my attorney was able to get me out on pretrial. While I was out, I managed to get my daughter some stuff before she was born. I then ended up in jail. Anyhow I felt like hope was gone.

Here I am almost halfway done with my sentence and my daughter was born May 2nd, 2020 one week after I got to the prison yard. When she was born, they found drugs in her system. APS got involved and placed my daughter with my fiance's mom. It scares me daily that I might lose my rights. I have not talked to my fiancé in seven months. It hurts but God is working in the situation. When I got to prison, I was lost without my family. I started attending church where Bob and Janene volunteer their time to come share God's word with us. I started focusing on what I can do instead of what I cannot do. I cannot change what I have done but I can make sure that my daughter never sees the old me. I have completed seventeen peer programs. I am currently on the Wild Fire crew.

I can call my daughter every Friday and CPS is going to bring my daughter to come see me every week. It is not me, but the Holy Spirit and my Lord Jesus Christ which makes this possible. When I got here my focus was that my daughter needs me. I know I cannot do this alone, but I can do all things through Christ who gives me strength. I never met my real dad and I work every day to make sure that does not happen with me and my daughter. I want to be a great father like God is to me.

This is May 1st. 2020, and the prison is still closed to us and to the families of the prisoners. The night before the prisons closed, we were given an option as to whether we wanted to cancel our service as other ministries did. We absolutely chose to trust God and do the service. That was a Friday night and on Saturday Randy was due to hold his ten-month old daughter for the first time. He worked for over a month to set this visit up and would pace the floor during the night with excitement to finally get to hold her. When we got news that the prison was closed to visitors, our heart was broken for R. The moment we are back as volunteers in Fort Grant, I hope to see a picture of him holding his little daughter.

Meet G

I am the son of immigrant parents who ventured to this country in hopes to settle in the comforts of the USA. I am forty-three years old. At a young age I began to experience and learn from life's hard lessons on what it means to lead a disobedient and unfruitful life. I took a turn that has caused havoc in my life as well as in the lives of my loved ones. I cannot say for certain where I went wrong but as hard as I tried to make things right it never turned out that way. By then I think I had just given up and yielded to the corrupt powers that were manifesting in my life. At twelve I began to experiment with drugs, mainly marijuana, but I soon enough was introduced to other drugs that just completely and all together devastated my life. I completely gave into violence, cheating, lying, and stealing.

I have been learning quite a bit about what it means to surrender these past couple of months and it has been a challenge for me. I sit, lay, or walk in my cell trying to figure out what it is that I am doing wrong. I have done roughly more than fourteen years in jails and prisons. Since accepting Jesus Christ as my Lord and Savior of my life I believe I understand what it means to surrender to God's Holy Spirit which is His gift to us through His beloved Son to help us live our lives in humble fellowship with our God. Which is why the Holy Spirit has blessed me with the privilege to share a revelation if you will of how futile it is as it has been for me, to restrain the Spirit of God from doing His work in and through our lives. May the Spirit of Wisdom open our eyes and mind and our hearts to receive His message with love and understanding. G

I was not able to write G's entire testimonial teaching he was expressing.

Meet E.C.

My name is E. C. I am thirty-nine years old. I was raised by a positive family. My mother was a single mom of four raising all of us to be good kids. Somehow, I chose to go a downward spiral at the age of fifteen hanging with the wrong crowds doing things I should not do. After seventeen-years of getting into trouble I was hit with a five-year prison sentence. At this time, I had three kids ages 3, 4, 5 and a wife when I was sentenced. I felt I was a failure to all the people I love. I had no faith and no one to turn to when times got hard in prison. After three months in prison my wife decided to move on and begin dating. It was then that I became angry and mad at the world. I felt I had no future and my life was over. I had hate, towards everything including my wife.

While in prison an older gentleman talked to me and told me to put the past behind me and look for God, kneel and pray for forgiveness. I did not know who was listening, but I knelt and prayed for to whoever was listening and told them I needed help, strength, and guidance. That same man also told me to forgive myself and release any ugly thoughts I had. He said to ask for help. After kneeling for the first time and praying I was able to feel as if my heart was lifted. I felt free and I knew God had taken the wheel. Unfortunately, after being released from prison I stopped prayers and forgot about faith. I went looking for my ex-wife and was determined to get her back even if it was not for my best interest. Six months after being released I was in trouble again and given three-and half-year sentence. I realized I lost faith, so again I knelt and asked the Lord for forgiveness and please guide me.

While I was fighting the case, I met a female who I knew was my soulmate. I felt this way because I loved her, and we were both lost and seeking guidance. We both discovered the love of Christ together. To this day she is my support and rock. We were both baptized around the same time. The Lord also blessed us with a baby girl. I still pray and ask the Lord to guide me. I attend church and it was in church where I was able to meet the Prudlers which has been a blessing and a life changer. So, I say to everyone, life is better and easier with God on your side.

Meet O

The Struggle is Real

These words are his testimony:

Pain and suffering, can you remember that one last meal. Making an attempt to smile, most recently has become for me a trial. Understanding the truth has been made difficult. Confused not yet introduced to the greatest of old, the greats of now and the greatest of later. This metaphoric dark hole as big as a crater. On my knees I give up, to You I surrender. Not sure of what to say, I began this prayer. Dear God, Hey, how are You? It is me down here. Ashamed of my ways, not too far from a tear. I want to be a better me, God I know that you are near.

Love, Joy, Peace and Patience are what I want to feel. As a grown man no longer a child, God, I just know that You are real. Please open my eyes to see the path I must take. Lord, help me with these things that I pray. Amen

Now Brother Bob has been coming for a long time sharing with us not only his time and love, but more of the word of God and God's love. Most recently explaining to us that he feels a strong presence of the Holy Spirit here on these yards. He has also spoken on the many different gifts that we all may have but may not be aware of. I believe deep inside we may all know what gift we are blessed to have. Only thing is, we need to ask God for a little bit more courage to produce. I say these things not to complain or disrespect, but more to say, "what are we waiting for." I hear a lot when I get out that I am going to do this or that to give back, again, "why wait?"

These gifts we have are bound to change the lives of those that are around us. Maybe more than we know. There are many that have a lot of unanswered questions, and we might just have the answers. Paul says in **Philippians 2:12-18**, and I also feel like Brother Bob says this to us all the time just by his presence here. Listen to your heart gentlemen, to the good that the Holy Spirit put in there. Not only when you are in His presence as we are now, but also throughout the rest of your days. Thank you for your time. C

Closing Reminder

THE TESTIMONIES AND PRAYERS you have read in this book are a witness that these men have not allowed their chains and circumstance to hold them back from the changes God desired to work in their lives. Until you put yourself in the presence of these prisoners you will have a difficult time seeing them not as criminals, but human beings that deserve another chance at life outside the walls that imprison them.

My prayer is that this book will inspire you to become a prison volunteer, and sow Christ's love into the men and women that are incarcerated.

Book Dedication

T**HIS** **BOOK** **IS** **BEING** **DEDICATED** to the Safford Prison Chaplains that are responsible for opening the doors for our team to minister in three Arizona Men's Prisons. During this Global Covid-19 Pandemic when volunteers were not permitted to return, Chaplain L. Chaplain R. and Chaplain C. were available to cover our services. Knowing that the prisoners were still being ministered to, certainly afforded us the peace we needed during this time. **1st Thessalonians 2:17-18** best expresses the way our hearts have felt over the past few months being unable to be with the guys we love. Paul says it perfectly. **But we, brethren, having been taken away from you for a short time in presence, not in heart, endeavored more eagerly to see your face with great desire. Therefore, we wanted to come to you, but we were hindered and could not.**

If it were not for the Safford Prison Guards and staff, we would never have succeeded in reaching the prisoners for Christ. Walking in and out of prison security gates and passing the guards has proven to be a positive experience for us as volunteers. This dedication truly extends to all of them, including the Warden and Deputy Wardens at Fort Grant, Tonto, and Graham Units. We want to express our thanks to all of you for making our ministry what it has been. We hope to continue this journey we are on.

Made in the USA
Middletown, DE
22 March 2021